CONTENTS

INTRODUCTION

Luna Lapin was a quiet and kind rabbit. All rabbits are quiet, so it was not this that made her exceptional. What made Luna exceptional was the way she always said hello to passers-by and, of course, her impeccable taste. Up until very recently she had lived in a warren in a sleepy little field somewhere far north. Her mamma often cooked soups in big black-bottomed pots, and her siblings hopped around laughing. Luna, however, was different. She liked to read and draw, she liked to pick flowers from the meadow, but more than anything she loved to sew, and she stashed fabric like squirrels collect nuts. Luna was never short of outfits to wear and garments flew from her sewing machine as fast as her nimble paws could make them.

This book shows you how to make a collection of Luna's lovely clothes, plus a dapper outfit for her brother Alfie.

M·A·K·I·N·G

LUNA
LAPIN

Sarah Peel

David and Charles

www.sewandso.co.uk

THE STORY OF LUNA LAPIN

I have always loved clothes – the shapes, the colours, the textures, and how the right outfit can change the day. I can get lost thinking about how clothing has evolved and the wide-ranging influences of current trends. I recognize the memories clothes can help to create.

As a child I was encouraged to sew my own clothes. As a teenager I studied the shapes of garment pieces by unpicking vintage and second-hand finds from jumble sales, and then tracing the patterns and re-sewing the garments. As an adult I was lucky to develop my career in the fashion industry, working as a pattern cutter, then as a buyer/designer. When I set up CoolCrafting, I felt the need to reintroduce clothing development and design into my business, and an achievable way of doing this was making patterns in miniature.

However, I needed a model, a muse for this project and the idea of a very well dressed rabbitty–hare was born. I knew the projects needed to be realistic and above all the rabbit needed to be loveable. With Liberty lined ears and long dangly limbs, Luna had to be achievable and easy to dress. She didn't take long to make, ending up 16in (40.6cm) tall, but it was a long time before the first sample was turned into a kit. The name came from the strange mix of features in Luna – the oversized ears reflected a hare, so I chose Luna (hares being associated with the moon). The rest of Luna was definitely rabbit and as she had a little French flair about her, it seemed right to be Lapin (French for rabbit).

The clothes were easy – the kind of capsule wardrobe perfect people have: a brightly coloured well-tailored wool coat, a classic, shaped dress in a ditsy floral. I enjoyed mixing textures of delicate lace with heritage tweed, styling a feminine dress with the edge and attitude of biker boots. As I introduced Luna and her wardrobe to the sewing community in the form of kits, I found everyone wanted Luna to have her own personality. Stories were formed and told, and the need for a pair of knickers became apparent as everyone lifted up her dress. As I find the right fabric, a new outfit is designed and drawn up. Alfie, Luna's brother, came along to introduce some menswear into this stylish miniature world.

Luna has been made and loved by many, many people around the world, especially in the UK. She isn't regarded as a toy; she is more of an heirloom piece, or an indulgence for all of us who are still children at heart.

Sarah

LUNA LAPIN AND THE LOST SCARF

Luna Lapin was a quiet and kind rabbit. All rabbits are quiet so it was not this that made her exceptional. What made Luna exceptional was the way she always said hello to passers-by and, of course, her impeccable taste. Up until very recently she had lived in a warren in a sleepy little field somewhere far north. Her mamma often cooked soups in big black-bottomed pots, and her siblings hopped around laughing. Luna, however, was different. She liked to read and draw, she liked to pick flowers from the meadow, she loved to sew and stashed fabric like squirrels collect nuts.

Luna sighed a sigh bigger than herself as she looked around her new, tiny but beautiful apartment, noting that all her lovely little things – cups and saucers, tiny paintings of seascapes and meadows she had yet to visit – sat in boxes waiting to be unpacked. A great armchair stood alone in the living room, surrounded by boxes of books and a suitcase. It was a shabby old thing, the arms worn away by elbows, and something like a coffee stain on the seat.

'What to do, what to do,' Luna muttered to herself before noticing the stack of fabric she had abandoned in the corner. A few hours and a battle to find matching thread later, Luna slumped down in her freshly covered armchair, its brand new cushion plumped to perfection. She let out a different kind of sigh and fell asleep. Sometimes home just happens, and sometimes we create it.

Luna woke up later than she had hoped, straightened her ears, fluffed up her tail and threw on her 'perfect for every occasion' dress, her 'no idea what else to wear' dress. Everyone should own a dress that makes them feel more like themselves. Luna's was prettily printed and ready for anything, including an interview for her first ever job. This particular dress was close to being Luna's favourite thing, but not

quite. By far Luna's favourite thing was her patchwork scarf. Her grandma had given it to her for her birthday two years ago and Luna was sure that it brought her luck. Today Luna needed luck. It was her very first day in the big city. Now rabbits don't like cities at the best of time, all that noise isn't nice for such big ears, and rush hour was definitely no exception, but Luna was an illustrator, and illustrators had to work in cities for a while. She took a deep breath wrapping the scarf around her neck.

'You've got this,' she whispered to herself, and with a click she walked out of the door.

Luna cycled everywhere. It was good for the environment and she liked the way the wind felt flowing past her ears. On most days it was lovely, but not when it rained and today was one of those days. The wind was blowing and Luna had to pedal twice as hard against it. But even in the rain Luna couldn't help but stop and gaze into the window of a department store. There was her perfect coat, woollen, with soft shoulders, deep pockets, and tiny buttons on the sleeve – the kind of coat that told people you had places to be. It came in the colour of faded hydrangeas, the pink of Turkish delight and the prettiest red Luna had ever seen. She gazed, sighed and turned her head. And with that the wind let out one fearsome gust, and with it went her scarf.

'Oooh, not today,' said one very soggy rabbit. 'Please, please not today.' But the wind doesn't listen to anyone, and Luna was too busy admiring the coat to notice her beautiful scarf had gone, and was sitting lonely in a large brown puddle.

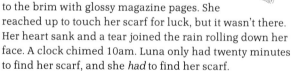

The huge, towering building that held the La Clairière offices was just ahead. Luna could taste a mixture of cold and excitement. She got off her bike and stared up at the tower of glass and metal. In her mind it was filled to the brim with glossy magazine pages. She reached up to touch her scarf for luck, but it wasn't there. Her heart sank and a tear joined the rain rolling down her face. A clock chimed 10am. Luna only had twenty minutes to find her scarf, and she *had* to find her scarf.

She looked around frantically and saw a flash of patchwork fifty feet away in a puddle. At that very moment the wind let out a howl and the scarf danced into the air. Luna ran after it. The wind took the scarf down the busy street, past passers-by too lost in the humdrum of Monday morning to notice the beautiful scarf or the rabbit chasing it. The wind seemed to laugh at Luna, throwing her scarf this way and that, until eventually it cast it aside onto the back of a fox rushing past. Luna summoned up all her courage and shouted to the fox, but he could not hear her and turned down to the underground. Luna would have missed him all together if it were not for the flash of his white-tipped tail.

By now Luna was sure her scarf was gone for good. The large clock above her ticked away, and with it her hopes of ever making it on time for her interview – just seven minutes left to get there. She sank onto a bench and buried her head in her hands. At the screech of a train she looked up. There was the fox climbing on board the very same train as her, with her scarf firmly clasped in his hand. Perhaps she would make her interview after all!

'Excuse me sir, you have my scarf.'

'This beautiful thing?' said the handsome fox. 'Why I was quite hoping it was my lucky day – it would have been perfect for a photo-shoot.'

'Can I have it back?'

'Why of course, though if you don't mind, could I borrow it? I'll have it cleaned. It's for La Clairière magazine, have you heard of it? I'm Ralph Reynard, the Editor in Chief.'

Luna's tiny heart skipped a beat. 'Oh, I'm going for an interview there! Only I'm late.'

'I'll tell you what,' he said, 'let me use the scarf and I'll walk you in personally. No-one can say you're late when you have been assisting the Editor in Chief, now can they?'

And with that they stepped off the train, arm in arm and headed for the La Clairière headquarters. Luna's lucky scarf certainly was lucky.

LUNA LAPIN AND THE CHRISTMAS WISH

Luna loved her job as an illustrator. She loved the way her pencil scratched on paper and the way colours moved and moulded into shapes and patterns. She loved the way designers and models chatted. She loved watching the make-up artists at work. She loved having lunch with Mae, who drank nothing but strangely aromatic green teas, laughed like a child and would excitedly grab her paw and drag her across the room if she spotted something interesting.

Mae always had the nicest things, mostly because her job as head stylist meant that she was sent the best of everything in the hope it would get featured. Luna wasn't the jealous kind, but there was a pair of soft brown boots in the corner of the bright white studio, which she knew were just her size. They were perfect, just below knee height, with a contrast lace. They were 'get up and go' boots, 'wear me anywhere' boots, 'woodland trek or second date' boots – the kind of boots you throw on with anything and suddenly the day is yours.

'You can have them if you like,' Mae smiled, 'but first I need you to do me a favour.'

Mae's ideas book was top secret, filled with next season and ten years in the future top trends. No-one got a peek into her private little world, not even Reynard. No-one that was, until Luna. Mae flipped open her book, quickly flicking through pages. Luna caught glimpses of oversized embroidery, too many colour swatches to count, ruffles, ricrac and pleats. Mae stopped on a two-page spread of

cut-outs of vintage-style French knickers.

'I can't find these anywhere and I need them for this shoot I have planned. You have to help me Luna!'

Luna got to work as soon as she got home, surprised at how easy it was to shape the lace into something beautiful and delicate; so easy in fact she made herself and Mae a pair too.

'They are perfect, Luna! I don't know how you do it,' Mae exclaimed as she examined the frills and the delicate little peach rose on the front. 'Please, take the boots, oh and this...' And like a fairy godmother she handed Luna a ticket to the most sought-after party of the year.

The La Clairière Christmas Party was the party to end all parties, an awards ceremony for the best dressed and most fabulous, but the awards were really hushed whispers and sighs of envy and admiration. And Luna had no idea what she would wear. She stared into her wardrobe for hours, ears alert, head cocked to one side.

'Why is it that as soon as your clothing becomes important, your coat hangers hold nothing but space and dust,' she thought to herself.

Early the next day Luna put on her very best winter shopping outfit, a beautiful tweed, A-line skirt, woven together with perfect pastels that danced and dipped through a blue as pretty as a cold sky. She had made it herself and had enough tweed left over to make a matching bag, just the right size for burrowing through charity shops and markets and hidden haberdasheries for treasures and long-lost things.

Luna's favourite haberdashery shop was on a tiny street that always felt like Christmas, and on this gloomy December day it felt even more magical than ever. The wide window with its grey paint looked more like heaven than anything as Luna's breath made excited smoke signals in the air. Inside there was felt in every imaginable colour, and a few she had not yet thought of. There was fabric in quirky prints and every possible polka dot, buttons that looked like flowers, horses and everything in between, and ribbons that made her heart sing. And then all of a sudden, with a twist of woollen red, the deep cherry red of Father Christmas himself, Luna fell in love. Inspiration had struck. She would make a red cape with holes in the hood for her ears, and a tiny bobtail trim around the edge. Under it she would wear a snow-white lace set with a full skirt that swished as she danced. Within ten minutes Luna's little bag was stuffed full of goodness and her bike basket brimmed with red as she pedalled home.

Luna's grandmother once said that every stitch is a story waiting to happen and Luna looked like a fairytale as she skipped into the dazzling lights of the ball. The room dripped with gold beads. Beautiful people, some wearing masks, danced around towering trees. Taffeta and tulle spilled out as Luna twirled through the crowds. This was as close to Venice of old as still existed, Luna thought. She glowed with pride as her outfit was admired by a crowd of people she had grown up longing to be a part of. A hand landed on her shoulder.

'Say hello to the big bad wolf,' Reynard purred, 'I think you deserve this.' He placed a delicate crown on her head. 'You look quite fantastic, Miss Moon.'

Luna caught her reflection in a giant gilded mirror that hung on the wall. He was right, she did look fantastic, oozing in confidence, her lace set just simple enough to scream style. The crown sat slightly off centre on her head. Luna felt regal, and in the company of great friends she danced and laughed and drank golden liquid from long-stemmed glasses that tasted like stars.

Much later that night, with sore paws from too much dancing, Luna flopped onto her favourite chair, happy to call the city home. She let out a little sigh of contentment and hopefulness for the New Year to come. She slipped out of her clothes into her strawberry-print pyjamas and drifted off to sleep, dreaming of eating wildflower salad amongst her brothers and sisters in their warm little burrow at home.

LUNA LAPIN AND THE BIG BIRTHDAY BASH

Luna had been dreading her birthday – the first she had spent away from home. She sat in her chair and flicked through old photos, gazing nostalgically at one photo. She was five, so small, with one ear still flopped over her face. Her mum had baked a huge carrot cake, decorated with cream cheese and five sparkling candles. Young Luna was wearing a polka dot coat dress with a white collar. That dress had climbed over a hundred trees and rolled down many a hill; it had been covered in grass stains and mud and fallen into one too many a river. But there, in the picture of her fifth birthday, it was brand new.

Luna's sewing machine winked at her from the corner of her apartment, inviting her to put a little more birthday cheer into her week. She set to work, digging out a pattern from a suitcase, rooting through her fabric stash to find the right cotton. And with a snip and a stitch and the whirr of her old machine, Luna got a little closer to feeling less lonely. A day and a decent night's sleep later Luna slipped on her new dress and twirled like she was five again. There was a knock at the door and Luna stopped twirling. She wasn't expecting anyone, who on earth could that be? She opened the front door – it was Alfie! She flung herself at her little brother.

'Alfie, I'm so glad you're here!' she laughed in delight.

'Hey, watch the waistcoat,' he chuckled, 'it's brand new.' Giving the wool a quick pat with his paw, he straightened out the check of his cotton shirt and then handed her two boxes.

Luna opened the first box, which housed a huge white-topped carrot cake! The second box was a slim rectangle tied with a dusky pink velvet bow edged with lace. Inside there was creamy tissue paper, layers and layers of it, and under it a beautiful wool coat. The same wool coat she had seen on the way to her interview.

'Oh Alfie, how did you know?'

Alfie, his head thrown back a little, laughed his usual casual laugh, deep and from the stomach. 'It's all you've talked about Luna... Go on then, put it on, we have somewhere to be.'

All Luna's friends were waiting for her in her favourite coffee shop down the road. It was only small, with high ceilings and low leather chairs, but they served great coffee, sandwiches on dense wholegrain bread and the most wonderful salted caramel brownies Luna had ever tasted. Mae, her favourite stylist, Reynard her good friend and editor, and many other familiar faces were all there for her, cappuccinos in hand.

'Sweetheart,' Reynard purred, 'we have something for you,' and he handed her the most beautiful piece of lace Luna had ever seen. It was a deep plum, with an intricate web of threads that created flowers weaving to and fro. Luna's quick little brain was already drawing out what she would make – a simple shrug to wear over all her best dresses.

Alfie smiled fondly at her. 'Do you love it? You love it, don't you? I knew she would. Didn't I tell you, Reynard?'

Luna looked over at her little brother, who had outgrown her some years ago. She was so proud and pleased to call him family. He shared her love of clothes and was always thinking of other people, ways to make them laugh, to light up their days. Not to say Alfie wasn't flawed; he used to put spiders in her bed and in one prank he'd tied her to a tree. Mostly though he was her little brother and the best rabbit she knew.

MATERIALS

This section describes the materials and equipment you will need to make the projects in this book. Many of the supplies you will need are available from CoolCrafting – see Suppliers for details.

BEFORE YOU START...

Before starting a project, look at the You Will Need list for the project and gather your supplies. Give yourself enough space and time to work – this really does help eliminate mistakes. Read through all of a project's instructions first and highlight any areas that you will need to focus on more than the simpler parts. Press fabric with a suitable iron temperature to ensure it is flat and easy to work with.

BASIC SEWING KIT

You will need some general supplies for making the projects in the book, including the following.

- Selection of needles, including sewing needle, tapestry needle, darner needle and doll needle (for sewing on arms)
- Sewing threads to suit projects, including embroidery threads
- Pins and safety pins
- Sharp scissors for fabric and scissors for paper
- Fabric marker (e.g. water-soluble marker or a chalk marker)
- Adhesive tape
- Implement for turning parts through and stuffing (e.g. knitting needle or chopstick)
- Iron
- Sewing machine

FABRICS

Various fabric types have been used for the projects in the book and this section gives some advice on using them. The fabric amounts needed for each garment are quite small, so generally no specific amounts are given.

Felt

Felt is possibly the perfect crafting material. The felt I am referring to in this book is a flat fabric-like felt, not what you would use for needle-felting or wet felting. Felt is not a woven fabric, but is formed by the agitation of fibres and therefore will not fray when you cut it. This allows you to cut a shape that can be appliquéd, or sewn to the outside of a project. However, not all felts are made equal, so if possible choose a felt that has wool in it, and look for a thickness of about 1.5mm (1/16in) – definitely no thicker. I adore the softly marled tones of the felts that are used for Luna and her clothes, which are a wool and viscose blend (see Suppliers). Felt doesn't have a grain to the material, so you can move your pattern pieces around to get the most out of your felt.

Wool Tweed

The beautiful soft colours and natural fibres of wool tweed make it perfect for Luna's fashionable wardrobe. Tweed is a heritage fabric and when buying it is worth researching the provenance of what you are investing in. Don't think you have to go out and buy a huge amount though – it may be you could recycle an old tweed jacket into a skirt and bag for Luna. Save scraps too, as the tiniest pieces can be used for appliqué. Avoid anything too chunky as Luna's clothes are a miniature scale, which means you need something mid-weight rather than heavy. If you are worried about matching stripes or checks, turn the fabric to be on the bias (so the pattern is diagonal) as this will give a different, less design-critical look.

Printed Fabrics

Cottons tend to be more stable than other fabric compositions and therefore will give you more control when you are sewing these small items. Choose prints that work with the scale of the garment – that's why I love the ditsy prints you will see in the projects. Choose fabrics that are lightweight without being delicate – a quilting weight is about as heavy as you should select.

Trims

There are some wonderful trims and haberdashery available, designed to make sewing easier as well as more beautiful. The most important consideration when choosing trims is scale: try to use doll buttons rather than those you would use for your own clothing. Select narrow ricrac or ribbon so it looks like it belongs in a miniature world. Be inventive – these designs are just a starting point and the best creations are of your own invention.

Lace

Lace is a delicate fabric and comes in all sorts of different compositions and therefore prices. Cotton lace is great for trimming clothing, whereas a nylon lace will have more drape and softness. I would tend to choose an ivory-coloured lace over white as it has a more vintage look. Charity (thrift) stores can be a great place to find old lace and don't be frightened to unpick precious lace off items that may be damaged elsewhere.

TIPS ON SEWING WITH LACE

When sewing lace, always check your sewing tension and iron temperature on a scrap of lace before you start your project. You may need to increase your stitch length on the sewing machine to 3.25 rather than the normal 2.75. If you are having tension issues (i.e. the lace is gathering up as you stitch), before you reach the end of the seam, pull the sewing out flat and it will take up some more top thread and relax the seam. You can then carry on sewing and reverse stitch at the end of the seam to secure.

When starting to sew a seam, start a little further in than normal, reverse for a couple of stitches and then stitch forwards again.

Holding on to the tail ends of thread firmly when starting out can avoid the lace disappearing into the hole below the sewing machine needle.

It can be difficult to see which is the right or wrong side of a lace, but just make sure you are consistent in your choice, and perhaps mark with chalk or small stickers.

TECHNIQUES

This section describes the basic techniques used for the projects. Each project is given a difficulty rating with the You Will Need lists – one carrot for easy projects, working up to three carrots for more difficult ones.

LAYOUTS

Layout diagrams are given for the projects as a guide for the amount of fabric needed, but if you have a different shape of fabric you will need to be flexible. Take note of which pattern piece will need to be cut out more than once and pin this onto double thickness fabric. The pattern pieces and layouts give this information so follow them carefully.

PATTERNS

All patterns are supplied full size in a section at the back of the book called The Patterns. Please follow the guidelines there for using the patterns.

CUTTING OUT

Time spent on accurate cutting will really improve your end result. Use a good quality pair of scissors that are suitable for (and reserved for) fabric. I tend to use the part of the blades that are closer to my hand to start cutting – this gives me better control and allows me to make a longer cut, as I have the rest of the blades to travel through the fabric. I only use the tips of the scissors when I am marking notches or for really fiddly bits.

TRANSFERRING MARKINGS

Mark the notches shown on the patterns with either a *tiny* snip in the fabric or using a water-soluble pen or chalk marker. Mark any triangles as a triangular cut from the fabric. Mark any dots on the patterns with either a water-soluble pen or tailor's tacks. The triangles and dots are position markers. The notches can be there to mark a position or to help you ease around curves so please be accurate when you are snipping them. Once you have marked the positions, unpin the pattern pieces from the cut fabric and store them together once you are sure you have cut them all out.

RIGHT SIDE AND WRONG SIDE

Printed fabrics and some plain fabrics have a right side and a wrong side, and this is shown in the illustrations and referred to in the instructions. With fabrics such as lace it can sometimes be difficult to see which is the right or wrong side – just make sure you are consistent in your choice, and perhaps mark with tailor's chalk or small stickers. Felt normally has no definite right or wrong side, but I have referred to right and wrong to help you sew.

FINISHING RAW EDGES

You could use an overlocker or a machine zigzag stitch to finish the raw edges of the seams on woven fabrics. The items in this book are small ones that are not going to be washed, so this is optional. Because of the nature of felt, the edges do not need finishing.

HAND SEWING STITCHES

Hand sewing is relaxing, portable and allows you to focus on something creative. Luna herself is sewn by hand and you could aim to complete a limb each night or perhaps take her on your commute to work. I have used various stitches, both practical and pretty. Always start and finish with either a knot in the fabric or a couple of small stitches in the same place.

Overstitch

I use an overstitch (also called slipstitch/whipstitch) to sew felt pieces together. Use a single thread thickness and make sure you sew consistently, that is, the same distance between stitches and the same depth in from the edge, about 2mm (1⁄16in) into the felt.

Bring the needle through to the front and then sew from back to front, repeating and working from right to left if you are right-handed or left to right if you are left-handed (see **Fig.1**). As you pull the thread through you will feel the tension as the thread is drawn and you can then continue to the next stitch. The thread will sink into the felt.

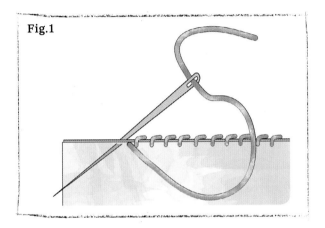

Fig.1

Backstitch

Backstitch is used to sew two pieces of fabric or felt together with a seam allowance. Backstitch is a good replacement for machine sewing if you wish to sew the garments by hand. Use a single toning sewing thread on your needle.

Following **Fig.2**, bring the needle up at point 1 and then back to point 2. Bring it out at the top again beyond point 1 at point 3, and then back through at point 4, which should be very close to or in the same place as point 1. Repeat along the seam.

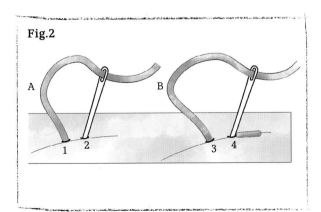

Fig.2

Blanket Stitch

Blanket stitch is a decorative and functional stitch that can be used to make a seam and to decorate it at the same time. The key to a good blanket stitch is consistency in the depth of the stitch and the distance between the stitches. A common mistake is to make the stitch too close to the edge of the fabric, which loses the decorative quality. Use a contrast embroidery thread to work blanket stitch – I tend to use between three and six strands of embroidery thread, depending on how bold you want the contrast stitch to look.

Following **Fig.3**, bring the needle through to front at point 1. Insert the needle in the front at 2 and come out at the back at 3, holding the thread under the needle at 3 as you pull the stitch tight.

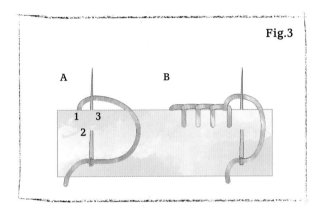

Fig.3

Herringbone Stitch

Herringbone stitch is a decorative and functional stitch that can be used to cover the raw edges of a hem, or purely as decoration. Stitches need to be even in size and placement. Use a contrast embroidery thread for decorative herringbone – I would use between three and six strands of the embroidery thread, depending on how bold you want the contrast stitch to look.

Following **Fig.4**, bring your needle up from the back to the front of the work at 1 and insert it back through the fabric at 2. Bring the needle to the front again at 3 and then down at 4 and up at 5, and so on.

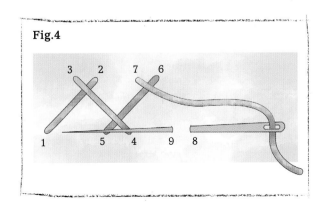

Fig.4

Satin Stitch

Satin stitch is an embroidery stitch that is good for creating blocked-out shapes in contrast colours. Use between three and six strands of the embroidery thread, depending on how bold you want the contrast stitch to look.

Following **Fig.5**, draw out the outline of the shape you are going to fill. Use the needle to pass backwards and forwards from outline to opposite outline. Try to keep your stitches parallel to one another and don't pull the stitches too tight.

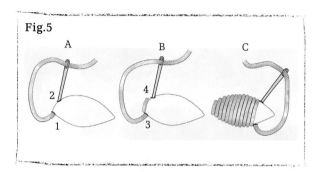

Fig.5

MACHINE SEWING TECHNIQUES

I recommend sewing the clothes for Luna and Alfie on a sewing machine as this will give a more professional and even finish. For these projects it is assumed that you have the basic skills of machine sewing. However, here are a few tips on how to sew small items.

The Right Stitch

Test your fabrics first, for example, a lace will react differently to a tweed under the machine and you may need to adjust the stitch length or tension.

'Donkey' or Stitch Starter

If you find that with small projects and fine fabrics your fabric tends to disappear down into the needle plate at the start of a seam, you could use what's called a donkey. Fold over a piece of scrap fabric so it's about 5cm (2in) square and a few layers thick and start your line of sewing on this. Butt the project up to the donkey and continue sewing onto the project – reversing as in Securing Your Stitching, below but without involving the donkey. You can snip the threads to detach the donkey at the end of the seam and use it again and again.

Securing Your Stitching

Always use your machine reverse function to start and finish seams as this will stop your seams from coming undone. The reversing should only be for two to three stiches – if you stitch any more than this then you probably will have lost the line of stitching anyway.

Seam Allowance

It is amazing how many people come to my Make Friends With Your Sewing Machine classes who don't know what the little parallel grooves are on the footplate of the sewing machine. These are your sewing guidelines and before you start sewing you should identify which line is right for the recommended seam allowance. So, if sewing with a 1cm (⅜in) seam allowance you should be feeding the sewing through the machine so the raw edges are on the right-hand side of the presser foot and are running along the 10mm groove. If you are working to a narrow 0.5cm (¼in) seam allowance use the edge of your presser foot as the guide for the edge of the fabric.

Using the Hand Wheel

Instead of using the foot pedal, using your hand wheel to make the last few stitches before a point you are aiming for can really improve your accuracy and confidence. Always turn the wheel towards you.

Turning a Corner

To make a crisp, accurate 90-degree corner when you are sewing, at the point of the corner leave the needle down in the fabric, lift the presser foot and move the fabric around at a 90-degree angle, and then continue sewing.

Coping with Curves

Sewing a curve is easier if you are using your seam guidelines. Slow down to control your sewing more easily and if you need to realign what you are doing, leave the needle down in the fabric, lift the presser foot and move the fabric slightly to bring the curve back in line. You may find that you have a speed setting on your machine or foot pedal, so if it helps you should slow the speed down whilst you practise new techniques.

Easing

There are times when it feels like you are squeezing more fabric on one side to match less fabric on another side. This can occur, for example, if you are setting in a sleeve or sewing a curve onto a straight piece of fabric. To help with easing there are two different techniques, as follows.

Method 1: This is the normal dressmaking technique. Change your stitch length to be the longest possible. Do not reverse at the beginning or end, and then on the longer looking side (normally the curved side), sew two rows of stitching. Row 1 should be 3mm (⅛in) from the raw edge. Row 2 should be 6mm (¼in). Now grab the sewing threads from one end of the upper side of the fabric and gently pull to slightly gather up the fabric. Do the same with the other ends, but make sure you don't have actual gathers, just more tightness. Now you can pin and sew to the other piece of fabric and eventually remove the initial stitching. Remember to change your stitch length back to normal first though.

Method 2: This is the factory method. Take the tighter (usually the straighter piece of fabric) and put snips 1cm (³⁄₈in) apart along the edge of the fabric, which are a little bit shorter than the seam allowance allowed. This will lengthen the edge of the fabric and allow it to stretch to the longer curved piece.

Edgestitching

An edgestitch is a line of stitching that is very close, about 1mm–2mm (¹⁄₃₂in–¹⁄₁₆in) away from a seam or folded edge. It is used to decorate or strengthen a seam. An easy way of establishing a guideline for edgestitching is to move your needle across to the left-hand position and then use the groove in the centre of the presser foot as your seam guideline. Stitch slowly to keep the stitching even.

Topstitching

A topstitch is a line of stitching that is close, about 4mm–5mm (³⁄₁₆in) away from a seam or folded edge. It is used to decorate or strengthen a seam. Use the edge of the presser foot as your seam guideline. Edgestitching and topstitching can be used together to create a twin needling effect.

Press As You Go

An iron is as valuable to the sewing process as the sewing machine itself. If possible, and depending on the shape, set the seam first by pressing the seam flat. Then open up the fabric and use the nose of the iron to either open up the seam allowances and press flat, or to flatten the seam allowances together in one direction. Your fingers will be working near the hot iron so do take care.

Making Buttonholes

Quite a few of the garments use buttons with buttonholes, although alternative instructions are given for using press studs. Most sewing machines have a buttonhole facility but it is a good idea to practise the technique on scrap fabric before you sew them on the actual garment.

A RABBIT

Luna felt fresh and clean after her bath, her bob tail fluffed up once more after a day making mud pies with her naughty little brother, Alfie. Granny pointed to her sewing machine and asked Luna if she would like to learn something new. Never one to shy away from new things, Luna nodded eagerly.

*Granny's sewing machine was a fine **old** thing. It sat amid **piles** of fabrics, **gleaming** black and **decorated** with a beautiful **trio** of flowers in **red** outlined with **gold***

YOU WILL NEED

- Paper pattern for rabbit (see The Patterns)
- Felt for body, 23cm x 91.5cm (9in x 36in)
- Liberty cotton fabric for ear lining and footpads, 15cm x 20cm (6in x 8in)
- Lightweight to mid-weight fusible interfacing for ears, 15cm x 18cm (6in x 7in)
- Two buttons for eyes and two buttons for arm joints
- Wool yarn for tail (optional)
- Toy stuffing, about 120gm (4½oz)
- Six-stranded embroidery cotton (floss) in brown for facial features
- Basic sewing kit (see Materials)

Before you start, refer to The Patterns section for advice on using the patterns.

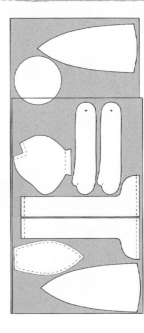

Fig.1

CUTTING OUT

1 Cut around the paper pattern pieces carefully. I cut on the black line, but to the outside not the inside.

2 Pin the rabbit pattern pieces onto the felt, using the layout in **Fig.1** as a guide. Mark any notches/triangles with a *tiny* snip in the felt. Unpin your pattern pieces. Cut out a pair of ears and a pair of footpads from the Liberty fabric. Mark the notches as before. Cut out a pair of ears from interfacing.

MAKING UP

Making the Ears:

1 Using an iron, fuse the interfacing to the wrong side of the print ears. Place the right side of a print ear onto one felt ear, matching edges and sew around the two edges 0.5cm (¼in) in from the edge, leaving the bottom open (**Fig.2**). You can machine sew or use a backstitch (see Techniques: Hand Sewing Stitches: Backstitch). Repeat to make the second ear.

2 Trim the seam allowance off at the points and then turn each ear through to the right side. Use a knitting needle or similar tool to carefully push the shape out. Roll the seams out to the edge between your fingers and press flat with a warm iron.

3 Sew through the ear layers to hold them together on a central line, trying to keep your stitches invisible on the felt side. Finish about two-thirds of the way up. Fold each ear in half lengthways, enclosing the print fabric (**Fig.3**), and pin in place.

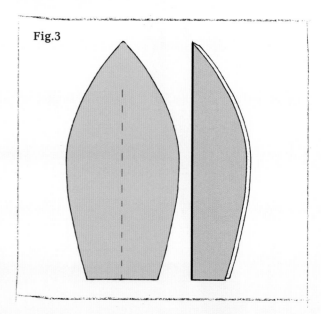

Fig.3

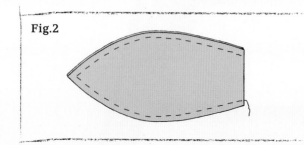

Fig.2

Making the Head:

1 Line up the bottom of an ear with the straight edge of a head piece, making sure the open (printed) edges of the ear are facing the nose. Fold the head piece over as in **Fig.4**. Make sure that the ear is tucked right up to the fold point. Sew through all layers 0.5cm (¼in) from the edge, on the sewing line. Use a backstitch or sewing machine for this stage. Repeat this step with the other ear and the other head piece, but the opposite way to the first one.

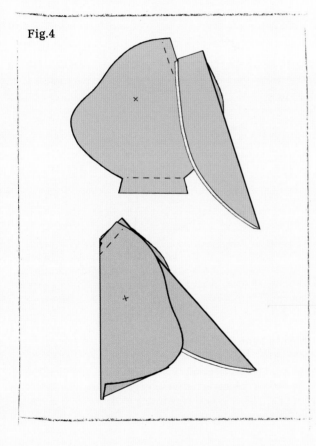

Fig.4

2 Turn the head pieces out to the right side and pin the centre front seams together so that the edges match. Oversew the two pieces together, leaving the neck opening free (**Fig.5**).

TIP
Practise your oversewing on some scrap felt before you start the rabbit, to get the stitches at the correct depth and distance. A polyester content sewing thread will have a bit more 'ping' or elasticity, allowing it to sink into the felt.

Fig.5

3 Stuff the head through the neck opening using small pieces of stuffing to build up the shape (**Fig.6**). Tuck the neck seam allowance up into the head.

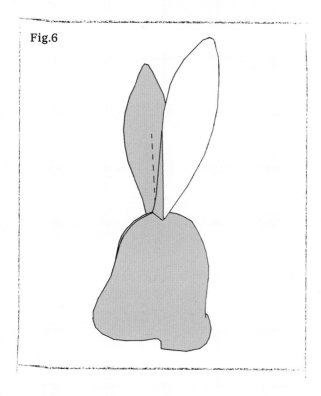

Fig.6

Making the Legs:

1 Oversew two leg pieces together down the long back seam. Starting from the foot, sew the front seam up to just over the foot (**Fig.7**).

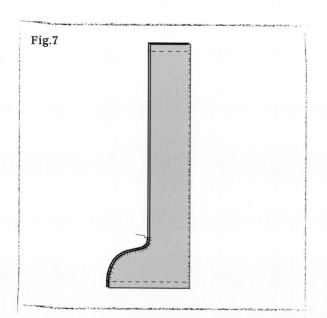

Fig.7

2 Now turn the leg so that these seams are to the inside and pin the footpad in place, using the notches on the foot pad to match up with the seams you have just sewn. Ease the footpad in place and sew 0.5cm (¼in) in all the way around using a backstitch (**Fig.8**). Turn the foot back out, so the raw edges are enclosed, and stuff the foot firmly. Resume oversewing the front leg seam, stuffing the leg firmly as you go. When you have completed one leg, repeat for the other leg. Leave about 1cm (⅜in) at the top with no stuffing. The legs should be the firmest stuffed part of the bunny (and the same length). At the top, fold each leg so that the front and back seams are in line with one another and either pin or sew flat.

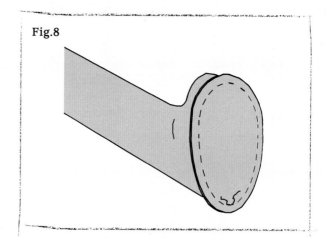

Fig.8

Making the Body:

1 Take two body pieces and oversew down one edge. Sew the third body piece onto another free side, and then join the two free seams at the lower edge and sew up about 5cm (2in) before fastening off (**Fig.9**). Turn inside out, so that the seams are to the inside ready for the next stage.

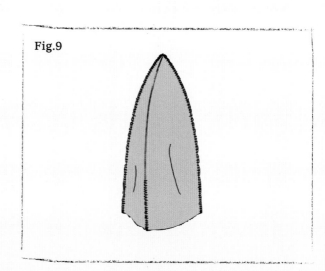

Fig.9

2 Push the legs inside the turned body. Position each flattened leg top so that the outside of the flattened leg is in line with a tummy seam, and so the toes are facing up towards the tummy. Sew in place using a backstitch or tacking (basting) stitch and a 0.5cm (¼in) seam allowance (**Fig.10**).

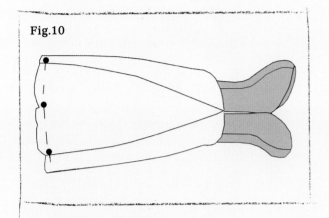

Fig.10

3 Take the circular base and matching up the three notches to the three seams of the body, enclose the raw edges of the legs and using a backstitch sew through all layers of the tummy, legs and base 0.5cm (¼in) from the edge (**Fig.11**). A double thread is better when sewing through four thicknesses of felt. Complete the sewing around the circle.

4 Turn the body back out so that the legs are dangling. Stuff and sew down the opening of the body, starting from the top and meeting up with where you had previously sewn. Make sure that you use enough stuffing for the body to be firm.

5 Check you have enough stuffing in the head, but still a gap for the point of the body cone. Push the point of the body cone into the head. Using a medium-size darner needle and double thread, sew the head to the body using a slipstitch and ensuring it is well attached by going around the neck at least twice (**Fig.12**).

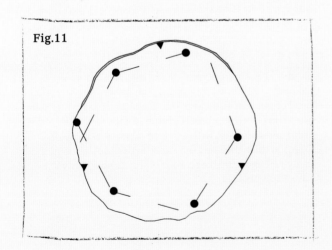

Fig.11

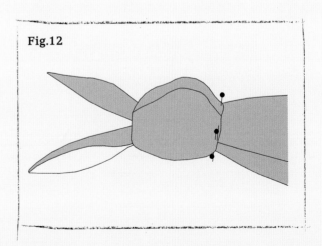

Fig.12

Making the Arms:

1 Match two arm pieces and sew together starting at the back of the arm. Oversew over the arm top, down the front and down to the hand (**Fig.13**). Use a deeper stitch to define the thumb and then oversew until you are 4cm (1½in) away from where you started.

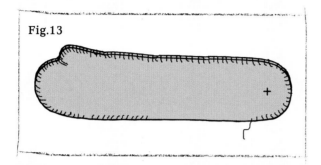

Fig.13

2 Stuff the arm firmly and then close the arm. Repeat this process to make a second arm.

3 Stitch the arms onto the body so that the top of the arm matches the level of the neck seam. Check you have the thumbs facing forwards. Position the buttons on the arms using the pattern piece as a guide. Use a double thread and the darner to sew the arms onto the body, going through the whole body and passing through the buttons on each side (**Fig.14**). Don't pull the arms in so tight that they change the shape of the body, but just enough to pull the arms in snug to the body. Secure by passing the needle through at least fifteen times – this needs to be secure as you will be moving the arms frequently to dress Luna.

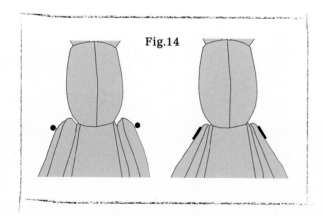

Fig.14

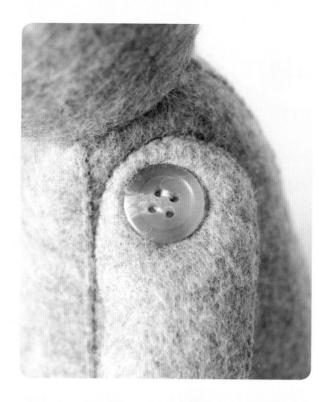

FINISHING OFF

1 Using three strands of brown embroidery thread sew on buttons for eyes in a similar way to the arms, checking the pattern piece for positioning. Add the eyes at the same time, sewing through the face, but this time pulling the eyes in slightly to indent the face a little. Use three strands of embroidery thread to satin stitch a triangular nose. The top of the nose should measure 6.5cm (2½in) from the ear / head seam. The nose should be about 1cm (⅜in) wide at its widest point. See Techniques: Hand Sewing Stitches for working these stitches.

2 Adding a tail is optional. Using the wool, make a pompom for the tail by winding the wool around a credit card or piece of stiff card. Snip down both edges and bind the centre with a remnant of wool. Shape and fluff up the wool and then trim with a pair of scissors to be about 2cm (¾in) in diameter. Sew the tail onto the back seam of the body just above the base. Your bunny is now ready to be loved and dressed.

HOW TO SEW LUNA'S

COMFY ARMCHAIR

Luna sighed as she looked around her
new apartment, at all her lovely things
still in boxes waiting to be unpacked –
still a great deal to do before it was home.
A great, shabby old armchair sat alone in
the living room. Nearby a stack of fabric
caught her eye and she had an idea...

Hours later, tired but contented,
Luna slumped down in her freshly
covered armchair, its brand new
cushion plumped to perfection.
Sometimes home just happens,
and sometimes we create it

YOU WILL NEED

- Paper pattern for armchair (see The Patterns)
- 100% cotton fabric, 35cm x 115cm (14in x 45in)
- Quilt wadding (batting)
- Foam, 5cm (2in) thick
- Stuffing, about 30gm (1oz)
- Glue gun
- Flexible plastic A4 (8¼in x 11¾in) size (e.g. a chocolate box lid)
- Basic sewing kit (see Materials)

Before you start, refer to The Patterns
section for advice on using the patterns.

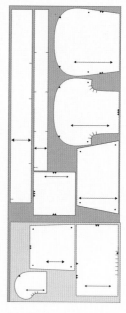

Fig.1

CUTTING OUT

1 Cut around your paper pattern pieces carefully. I cut
on the black line, but to the outside not the inside. On
the long lower panel, join parts A, B and C using adhesive
tape. For the long side panel, join parts A and B. When
preparing the fabric for cutting have it facing upwards
and fold over one selvedge edge by about 25cm (10in)
to give an area where you can cut the pieces out on the
doubled up fabric.

2 Pin the pattern pieces onto the fabric, using the layout
in **Fig.1** as a guide. Cut out the pieces. Mark the notches
shown with either a *tiny* snip in the fabric or using a
water-soluble pen or chalk. Mark any triangles as triangles
cut from the fabric. Mark dots on the patterns with a
water-soluble pen or tailor's tacks. The triangles and
dots are position markers. The notches will help you ease
around curves so be accurate when snipping them. Unpin
the patterns from the cut fabric. The fabric has a right and
a wrong side (shown in the diagrams and referred to in
the instructions). A 1cm (⅜in) seam allowance is used for
this project.

TIP
You could try different
fabrics for this chair – it
would look great in jacquards
or tweed. You could also
patchwork the chair to create
a very on-trend look. Adding a
bobble trim or tassels around
the lower panel would give
it a different look.

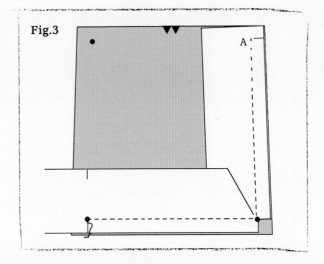

Fig.3

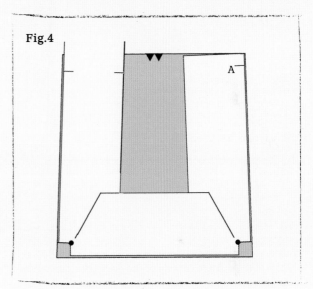

Fig.4

MAKING UP

Making the Box Cushion:

1 The long strip (side panel) has notches marked along it. Find the edge that has a snip 1cm (⅜in) from the short edge (marked A). With this as the starting point and with right sides of the fabric together, match to the corner marked A on one of the top/base pieces. Starting 1cm (⅜in) from the edge, at the level of the snip, sew down the long edge to the dot at the next corner. This should line up with the snip in the long strip (**Fig.2**). Leave the needle in the machine, lift the foot and turn the long strip to 90 degrees, then pivot and line up the next edge. The snip next to your pivot will open up. Stitch along this edge and pivot at the notch (**Fig.3**). Continue along the remaining two edges, making sure when you are on the last edge that the start of the side panel is out of the way (**Fig.4**).

2 To complete the side panel, pin the two short edges of the side panel and sew together, starting 1cm (⅜in) from the edge. Pin together and then sew up the short edges of the side strip (**Fig.5**).

Fig.2

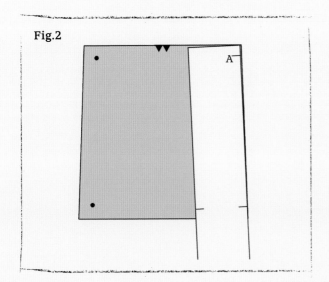

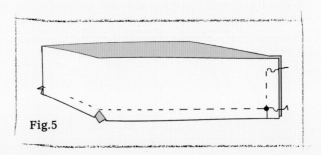

Fig.5

3 Take the remaining cushion piece and match it to a long edge of the side strip and repeat, as above, *but* leave the last double-notched edge open in order to turn and fill the cushion (**Fig.6**).

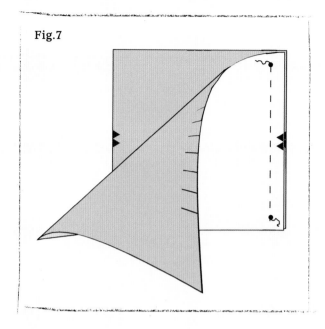

Fig.7

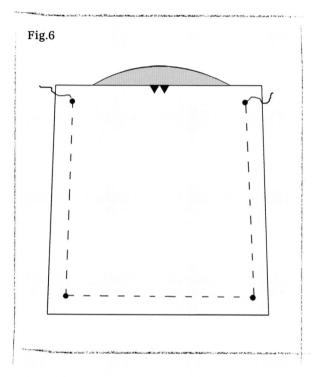

Fig.6

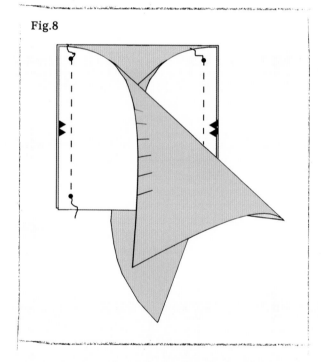

Fig.8

4 Turn the cushion right sides out. Fill it with stuffing and then pull the outside corners of the open edge outwards, to help the seam allowance turn in. Slipstitch the two edges together, to seal the cushion.

Making the Chair:

1 Attach the seat square to the overarm panels as follows. Place the seat square right side up, notch free along the top and with the triple notch at the bottom. Take the two overarm panels, find the edge with many notches along it and make sure that edge is at the top. Match a short edge with a double notch on to the seat square. Starting 1cm (⅜in) in and finishing 1cm (⅜in) from the edge, sew down this seam (**Fig.7**). Repeat with the other double-notched side of the seat square and the other overarm panel (**Fig.8**). Press seams open and flat (**Fig.9**).

Fig.9

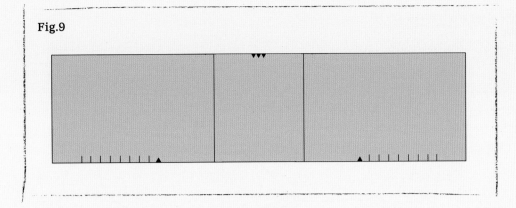

2 Prepare the arm ends and overarm panel as follows. Lay the continuous overarm/seat piece in front of you with the right side of the fabric facing up. Lay the two arm ends right side down, as shown in **Fig.10**. Pin both sides temporarily in the right direction as you focus on attaching just one side.

Fig.10

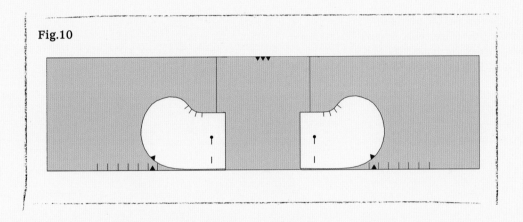

3 Sew the arm ends onto the overarm panels as follows (this can be a bit tricky). Overlap the arm end seam by 1cm (⅜in) past the seam, and then match and pin the overarm panel to the curves of the arm end – the multiple notches you have made in the fabric will allow you to ease in the curves. Tack (baste) if you like and then sew (**Fig.11**). Don't allow the curves and easing to distract you from the 1cm (⅜in) seam allowance you should be stitching to. Avoid going narrower and, if necessary, put the needle down in the fabric, lift the foot and pivot the fabric a little to maintain the curve.

Fig.11

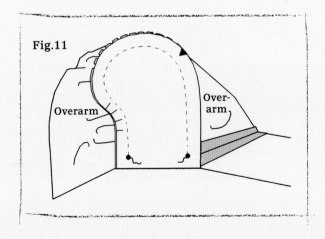

Overarm

Over- arm

4 Repeat this process with the other arm end and the other overarm seam (**Fig.12**).

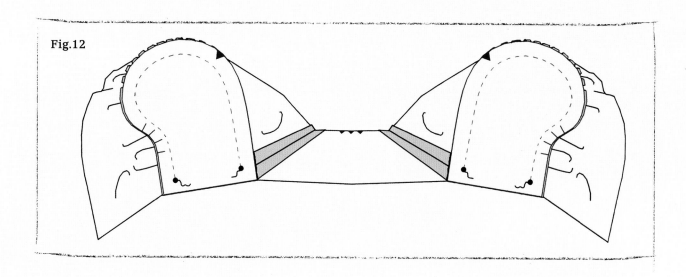

Fig.12

5 Sew the seat panel to the upper back as follows. With right sides together and matching the triple notch, positon the seat edge up to the lowest edge of the upper back. Sew but remember to start and finish your seam 1cm (⅜in) in from the ends (**Fig.13**).

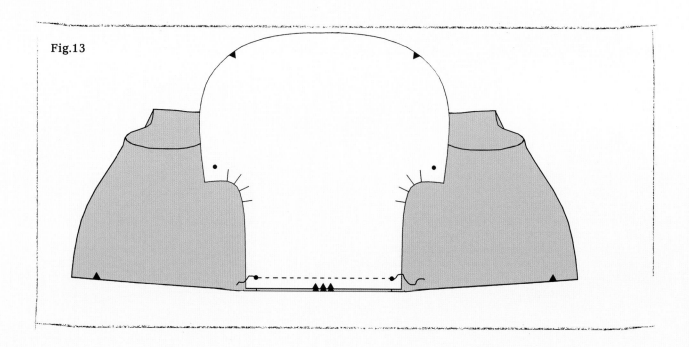

Fig.13

6 Sew the overarm panel to the upper back as follows. Working one side at a time and with right sides together, match the overarm panel up to the curved edge of the upper back. Aim to match the notch on the overarm panel to the dot on the upper back panel. Pin as far as the marked dot on the overarm panel and use the notches on the curve to ease around the curve. Sew from 1cm (⅜in) up from the edge to the notch/dot point, which is 1cm (⅜in) in from the end of the upper back (**Fig.14**). Repeat with the other side.

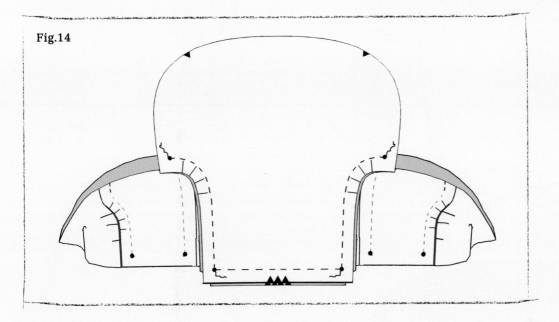

Fig.14

7 Sew the curve on the upper back to the full back panel. With right sides together, match the upper back to the full back panel between the marked dots, and sew together around the curve (**Fig.15**).

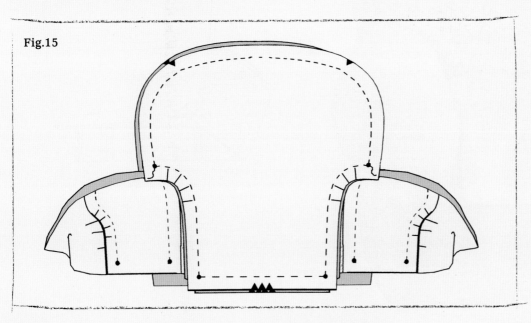

Fig.15

8 Sew the full back panel sides to the overarm panels as follows. With right sides together, match the remaining free edges – below the marked dot on the full back panel, to the remaining free edge of the overarm panel. Sew together, starting at the level of the marked dot / notch (**Fig.16**). Repeat with the other side and then turn through. If the shape was stuffed it would look like **Fig.17**.

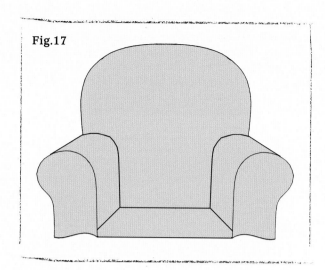

Fig.17

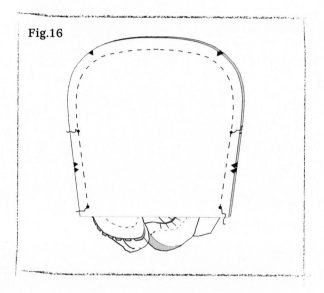

Fig.16

9 Attach the lower panel to the upper chair as follows. Imagine you are sitting in the chair and put a pin in the back left-hand corner. Take the long strip and with right sides together, find the notch marked Z on the pattern and match it to the corner you put a pin in (**Fig.18**). Pin and then sew the long strip all around the lower edge of the chair, finishing 1cm (⅜in) from the end of the strip when you are all the way around. This should match up to the seam where you started.

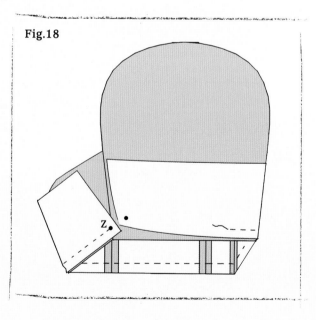

Fig.18

10 Take the two short edges of the lower panel and pin, then sew together, starting 1cm (⅜in) from the edge (where you can see your other stitching starts or finishes). Pin together and then sew up the short edges of the side strip (**Fig.19**).

11 To attach the chair base take the base and starting at one of the back corners, pin and then sew the base onto the lower panel, starting 1cm (⅜in) away from the edge (**Fig.20**). Use the notches in the long strip to turn the corners. Leave the back edge open to be able to fill and stuff the chair later.

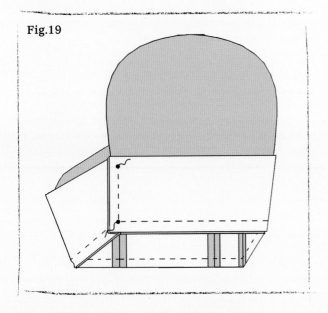

Fig.19

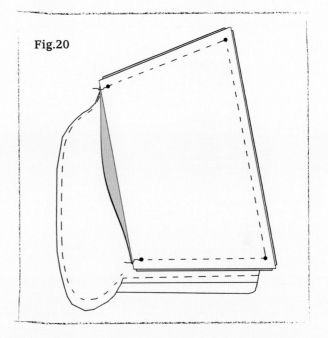

Fig.20

TIP
The hollow fibre found in supermarket pillows makes an economical alternative to toy stuffing.

12 To make the flexible back panel, trace the template onto a piece of flexible plastic. Using a glue gun, glue some stuffing onto one side of the curved edge of the plastic (**Fig.21**). When it is set, pull over the back and glue in place to create a slightly padded effect. Bend the panel slightly to slide it into the fabric shell through the opening in the base.

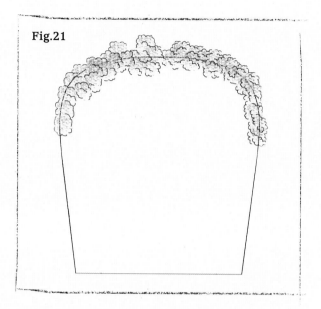

Fig.21

13 To make the arm rolls take the wadding (batting) and cut two pieces to be 57cm (22½in) long x 10cm (4in) wide. Roll each piece up and either hot glue to secure or stitch it lightly in place (**Fig.22**). Push a roll into the top of each arm of the chair and wedge up against the back panel.

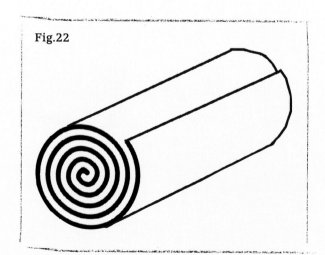

Fig.22

FINISHING OFF

1 Use the pattern for the chair base to draw onto the foam pad. Include the seam allowance – you want the chair to look packed. Cut out the shape using strong scissors, trying to ensure your cut is at right angles to the surface. Push the widest end into the chair base first and wriggle everything around until you have an accurate, snug fit. As a minor adjustment I pushed some extra stuffing between the arm rolls and the foam pad at the front as I felt they needed a bit more rigidity/height.

2 You could sew through the deepest inner corners of the seat to the back corner seam on each side to create a tidy space in the deepest part of the chair. Use a double thread for strength (**Fig.23**). Finally, turn in the seam allowances of the open edges at the back of the chair base and slipstitch the opening together. If Luna is sitting in the chair you will find she looks better without the box cushion in place.

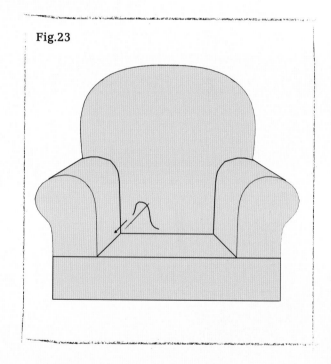

Fig.23

HOW TO SEW LUNA'S

T-SHIRT DRESS,
LACE SHRUG,
FRENCH KNICKERS
AND SHOES

All Luna's friends were waiting for her
in the coffee shop, including Mae, her
favourite stylist, and Ralph Reynard,
her editor. Smiling, he handed her a
birthday gift, the most exquisite piece of
lace. Luna's quick brain began planning
what she would make – a gorgeous shrug
to wear over all her best dresses!

It was the most **beautiful** piece of

lace Luna had ever seen,

a deep **plum**, with an **intricate**

web of threads that created

flowers as they **wove** to and fro

THE T-SHIRT DRESS
YOU WILL NEED

- Paper pattern for T-shirt dress (see The Patterns)
- Liberty fabric, 38cm x 71cm (15in x 28in)
- Two tiny buttons
- Two press studs
- A badge pin
- Basic sewing kit (see Materials)

Before you start, refer to The Patterns section for advice on using the patterns.

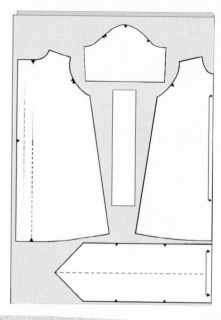

Fig.1

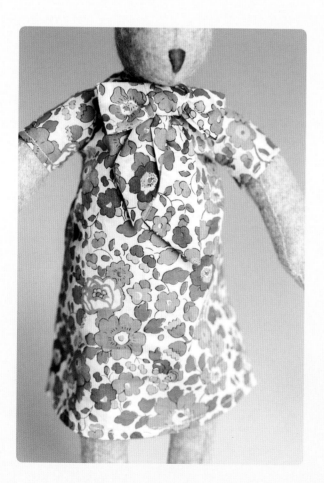

CUTTING OUT

1 Cut around your paper pattern pieces carefully using scissors. I cut on the black line, but to the outside not the inside.

2 Fold the Liberty fabric in half so that right sides are together and short edges match. Pin your pattern pieces onto the fabric, using the layout in **Fig.1** as a guide. Cut out the pieces carefully. Mark any notches/triangles shown on the pattern with a *tiny* snip in the fabric to the centre of the triangle.

TIP
Fabric choice is critical to the success of your end result. Standing a few metres away from your choice of designs will give you a better impression of how they will look when completed.

MAKING UP

1 Use a zigzag stitch to finish the raw edges of the long back edge. With right sides together, pin the two back pieces together and sew 2cm (¾in) in from the edge, from the snip to the hem (**Fig.2**). Press both seam allowances to the right, all the way up to the snip at the neckline. On the left back press 1cm (⅜in) of the seam allowance back on itself, as shown in **Fig.3**.

2 With right sides together, match the front and back pieces at the shoulder seams. Sew together with a 0.5cm (¼in) seam on each side (**Fig.4**). Press towards the back.

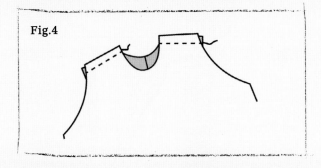

Fig.4

3 Using an iron, turn up the sleeve hems by 0.5cm (¼in) and then again by the same amount and edgestitch in place (**Fig.5**).

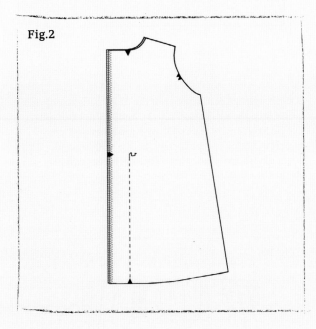

Fig.2

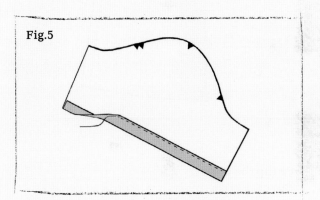

Fig.5

4 With right sides together, and using the snips to position, pin and sew the sleeves onto the dress using a 0.5cm (¼in) seam allowance (**Fig.6**). You may need to keep your needle down and adjust your fabric to turn and sew the curves of the seam. Press the seam allowance towards the dress body.

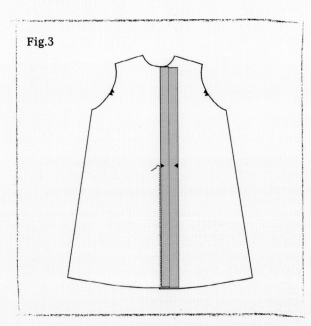

Fig.3

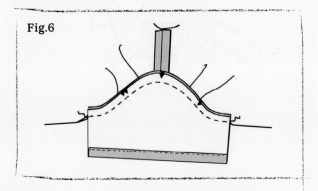

Fig.6

5 With right sides together, match up the sleeve seams, underarm and side seams and pin in place. Sew 0.5cm (¼in) away from the edge as in **Fig.7**. Press seams towards the back of the dress as far as you can. Snip the fabric once at the underarm and turn the dress inside out.

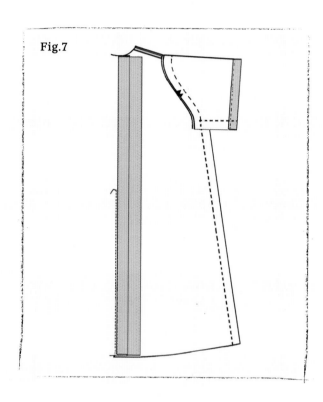

Fig.7

Sewing the Collar:

1 Staystitch 0.5cm (¼in) in from the edge of the neck, using a long stitch so it can be easily removed. Snip into the fabric where the curves are tight on the neck but don't cut past the staystitching (**Fig.8**).

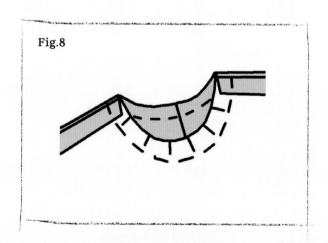

Fig.8

2 Prepare the collar by turning in 0.5cm (¼in) to the wrong side on one edge of the neck strip and use an iron to press in place (**Fig.9**).

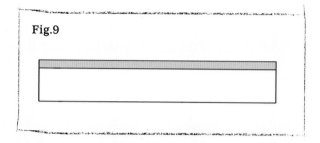

Fig.9

3 With right sides together, pin the unturned edge of the collar onto the neck edge. Leave 0.5cm (¼in) extending over at each end of the collar when you position the neckline as this will be turned in. Sew with a 0.5cm (¼in) seam allowance – the snips in the neck edge will give you the ease to sew in the collar strip (**Fig.10**).

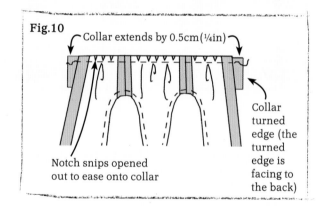

Fig.10

Collar extends by 0.5cm(¼in)

Collar turned edge (the turned edge is facing to the back)

Notch snips opened out to ease onto collar

4 Using an iron, press the seam allowance away from the dress and towards the collar. Trim the allowance back to 3mm (⅛in) and then press the collar in half, so that the previously pressed edge matches the line of stitching.

5 Turn the ends of the collar in and slipstitch in place. Slipstitch the inside down and remove the staystitching. Sew the buttons in position at the back of the dress on the left-hand side, positioning one on the collar and one 4cm (1½in) below. Position a press stud below the button and sew directly under, with the matching press stud component on the right-hand side of the dress, facing out.

6 Using an iron, turn up the dress hems by 0.5cm (¼in) and then again by the same amount. Edgestitch in place.

Making the Detachable Bow:

1 Fold the bow in half so that right sides are together and long edges match. Using a 0.5cm (¼in) seam allowance sew from one point to the snip, and then from the other point to the other snip, leaving a 4cm (1½in) opening to turn through (**Fig.11**). Trim excess seam allowance away from points and turn through using a knitting needle to push the corners out. Roll the seams out to the edges between your fingers and press flat. Turn in the seam allowance on the turning opening and slipstitch closed.

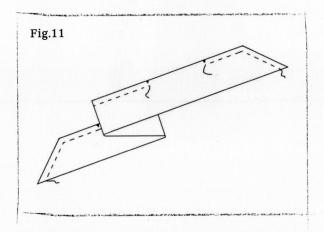

Fig.11

2 Measure in 8cm (3¼in) from one point and fold (A). Fold again 4cm (1½in) further away in the opposite direction (B), then at 8cm (3¼in) further on (C), and again 4cm (1½in) along (D) (**Fig.12** and **Fig.13**). Use a gathering stitch (**Fig.14**) to draw the bow up in the centre of each side but don't get the tails involved (**Fig.15**).

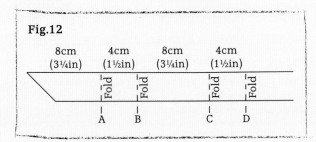

Fig.12

8cm (3¼in)	4cm (1½in)	8cm (3¼in)	4cm (1½in)
	Fold	Fold	Fold	Fold
A	B		C	D

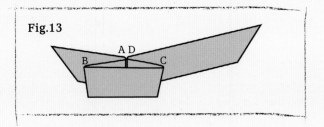

Fig.13

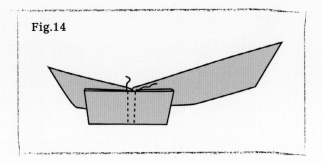

Fig.14

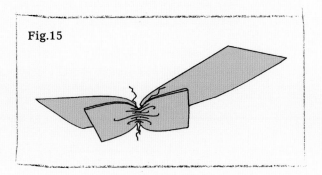

Fig.15

3 Flip the work to the back. Fold the tails flat and then wrap the longer one around from under to over, making a loop that covers the gathering stitches (**Fig.16**). Sew the wrap of the bow down to secure. Slip the badge pin back through the loop at the back and tighten the opening with a few stitches to secure (**Fig.17**). Pin to the front of the dress just below the neckline. Well done – time to get Luna dressed!

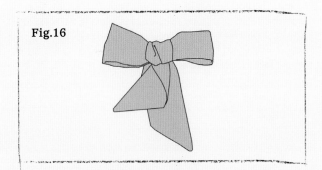

Fig.16

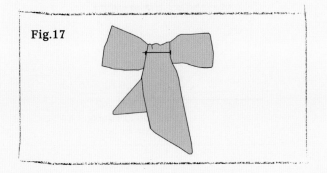

Fig.17

THE LACE SHRUG
YOU WILL NEED

- Paper pattern for lace shrug (see The Patterns)
- Lace with scalloped edge, 1m (1yd)
- Basic sewing kit (see Materials)

Before you start, refer to The Patterns section for advice on using the patterns.

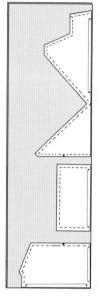

Fig.1

CUTTING OUT

1 Cut around your paper pattern pieces carefully. I cut on the black line, but to the outside not the inside.

2 Fold the lace in half so right sides are together. Ensure that the scallop shapes at the bottom edge of the lace match up with one another. Pin your pattern pieces onto the fabric, using the layout in **Fig.1** as a guide. The most important area to position is the middle of the front where the stitching will come down to the edge. Position this so that it is in a deep scallop (**Fig.2**). Position the sleeves so that each short edge falls at a similar position on the lace, and the sleeve seams are the same length (**Fig.3**). Position the back on a fold so the side seams are falling on the same scallop depth (**Fig.4**). To mark a notch, cut a *tiny* snip in the lace to the centre of the triangle.

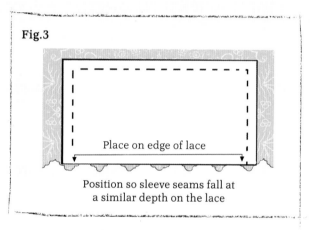

Fig.3

Place on edge of lace

Position so sleeve seams fall at a similar depth on the lace

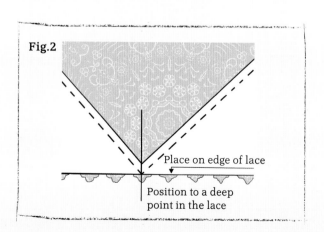

Fig.2

Place on edge of lace

Position to a deep point in the lace

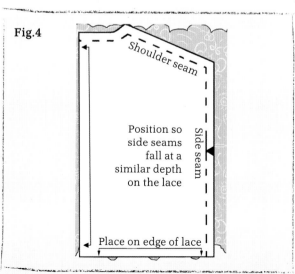

Fig.4

Shoulder seam

Side seam

Position so side seams fall at a similar depth on the lace

Place on edge of lace

MAKING UP

1 See Materials: Lace, for tips on sewing with lace. Take a front piece and fold it over to match the central V, ensuring right sides are together (**Fig.5**). Sew from the narrow part using a very small seam allowance and increasing to a 0.5cm (¼in) seam allowance (**Fig.6**). Repeat with the opposite side, taking care to end up with two different sides. Press seams downwards.

3 With right sides together, match the shoulder seams of one front to one side of the back, and sew using a 0.5cm (¼in) seam allowance. Sew from the edge of the sleeve seam and finish 0.5cm (¼in) before the end of the neck seam (**Fig.8**). You can see where you should finish by referring to the dashed guidelines on the pattern. Press seams towards the back.

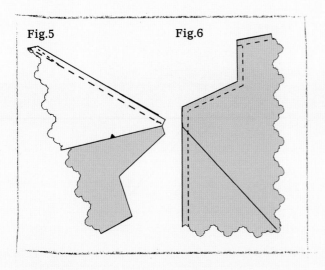

Fig.5   **Fig.6**

Fig.8

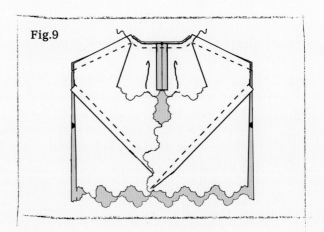

2 With right sides together, match the front pieces at the back neck and sew a 0.5cm (¼in) seam (**Fig.7**). Press seam allowances open.

4 Match the back neck edge up to the front neck edge. Starting from where you finished sewing the shoulder seam, sew with a 0.5cm (¼in) seam allowance to meet the other shoulder seam (**Fig.9**). Press the seam towards the body of the shrug.

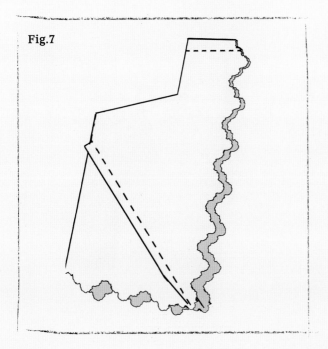

Fig.7

Fig.9

5 With right sides together, position a sleeve over the front/back piece, matching up the notches where the sleeve piece should finish. Sew with a 0.5cm (¼in) seam allowance, starting and finishing 0.5cm (¼in) in from the ends of the sleeve (**Fig.10**). Press seams towards the sleeve and away from the body. Repeat with other side.

6 Match the sleeve seams together with the side seams and sew from the sleeve hem up to the underarm point using a 0.5cm (¼in) seam, and then, with your needle down, lift the presser foot and pivot to continue sewing down the side seam to the hem (**Fig.11**). The flexibility of the lace will allow you to stretch one side a little bit if you find that your lace pieces are not matching perfectly. Press side seams towards the back of the garment.

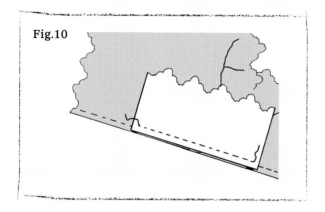

Fig.10

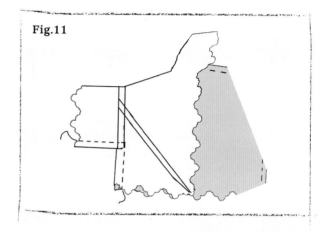

Fig.11

7 Turn the garment through to the right side, trim all loose ends and pop the shrug on Luna over her favourite dress.

THE FRENCH KNICKERS
YOU WILL NEED

- Paper pattern for French knickers (see The Patterns)
- Lace with scalloped edge, 15cm (6in) wide x 60cm (24in)
- Elastic, 0.5cm (¼in) wide x 22cm (9in)
- A small lace motif
- Safety pin
- Basic sewing kit (see Materials)

Before you start, refer to The Patterns section for advice on using the patterns.

CUTTING OUT

1 Cut out the pattern pieces, laying the lowest edge of the pattern on the bottom edge of the lace. See also Materials: Lace, for tips on sewing with lace.

MAKING UP

1 With right sides together, match the inside leg seams and sew using a 0.5cm (¼in) seam allowance (**Fig.1**).

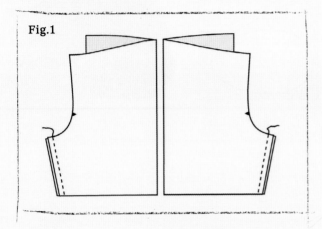

Fig.1

2 To sew the crotch, turn one leg right side out and slide it, lower edge first, inside the other leg. Matching the edges and inside leg seam, pin and sew the crotch with a 0.5cm (¼in) seam allowance (**Fig.2**).

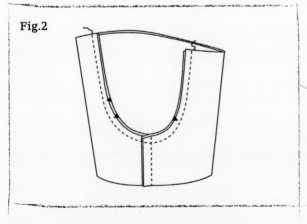

Fig.2

3 To make the casing for the elastic, turn down the top edge of the waist by 1cm (⅜in) and then another 1cm (⅜in). Sew close to the folded edge, starting at the centre back and finishing about 1cm (⅜in) from where you started stitching. This will leave an opening for threading the elastic. Sew around the top edge close to the fold all the way around (**Fig.3**). Put a safety pin through one end of the elastic and close the pin. Thread the elastic through the casing, ensuring that the unthreaded end of the elastic is still accessible.

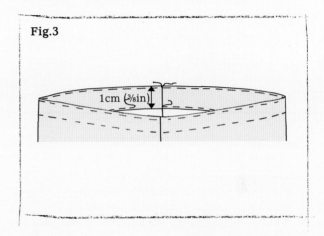

Fig.3

1cm (⅜in)

4 Adjust the gathering around the waist to be even and trim 2.5cm (1in) off the end of the elastic. Overlap the two elastic ends by 2.5cm (1in) and join together using a machine zigzag stitch. Pull the waistband out so the ends of the elastic disappear into the casing. Close the casing opening with machine stitching. To finish, sew on the lace motif just below the elastic at the centre front.

THE SHOES
YOU WILL NEED

- Paper pattern for shoes (see The Patterns)
- Wool felt, 16.5cm (6½in) square
- Six-stranded embroidery cotton (floss)
- Two press studs
- Two tiny buckles (or decorate with tiny buttons)
- Basic sewing kit (see Materials)

Before you start, refer to The Patterns section for advice on using the patterns.

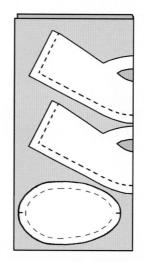

Fig.1

CUTTING OUT

1 Cut around your paper pattern pieces carefully. I cut on the black line, but to the outside not the inside. Seam allowances are included.

2 Pin the pattern piece for the top of the shoe onto the fabric, using **Fig.1** as a guide. The pattern is placed on the fold so it is easier to cut out the front. Mark the centre front and any notches shown on the pattern using a water-soluble marker or chalk. Unpin your pattern piece from the cut fabric and repeat to cut a second shoe piece. Cut the sole on double thickness.

MAKING UP

1 These shoes are sewn by hand. Because of the nature of felt, the edges of the fabric do not need finishing. There is no definite right or wrong side to felt, but I have referred to right and wrong to help you sew. These instructions describe making one shoe at a time – you could work this way or repeat each step and make up both shoes together.

2 To make the straps, lay the two shoe shapes open in front of you and cut through one edge of the strap on each piece – you will need to do this on opposite sides so they end up being for a right foot and a left foot (**Fig.2**). Gently stretch the free end of each strap so that it becomes 0.75cm–1cm (⁵⁄₁₆in–³⁄₈in) longer than it was originally (**Fig.3**).

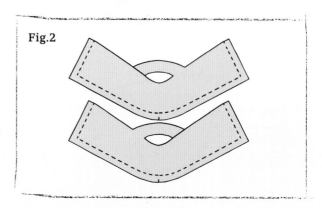

Fig.2

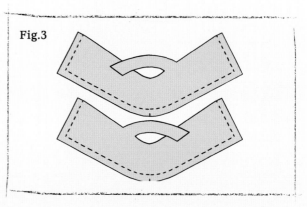

Fig.3

3 Embroider the shoe top using all six strands of the embroidery thread, sewing a decorative running stitch around the top edge of the shoe and the strap (**Fig.4**). You could use blanket stitch if you prefer. Now make a hole in the strap with the end of a large needle and rotate it to enlarge the hole. The hole should be 1.5cm (⅝in) from the centre of the end of the strap (**Fig.5**).

5 To sew the back seam, turn the shoe so right sides are together and the two back edges are matching. Sew together with a 0.5cm (¼in) seam allowance and backstitch with two strands of embroidery thread (see Techniques: Hand Embroidery Stitches: Backstitch) (**Fig.7**). Finger press the back seam allowances open.

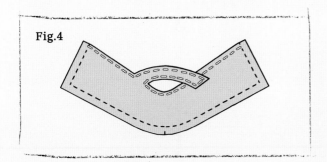

Fig.4

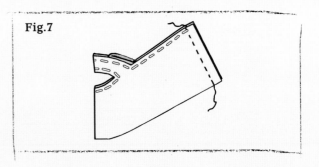

Fig.7

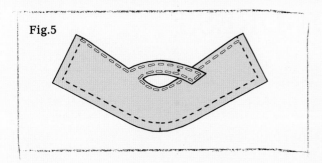

Fig.5

6 Attach the shoe to the sole as follows. With wrong sides together, match the mark at the front of the shoe to the sole notch, and the back seam to the other sole notch. Tack (baste) the sole onto the shoe, easing the felt in as necessary. Using six strands of embroidery thread, sew the shoe to the sole using a blanket stitch (**Fig.8**) about 0.5cm (¼in) deep (see Techniques: Hand Embroidery Stitches: Blanket Stitch). Remove any tacking threads.

4 Take the end of the buckle with the prong nearest to it and thread the felt strap under the end bar. Push the prong upwards through the hole and then thread the strap end under the opposite end bar (**Fig.6**).

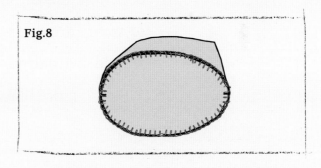

Fig.8

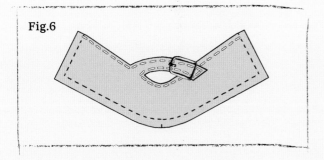

Fig.6

7 Try the shoes on Luna's feet and mark a position where the strap sits over the shoe. If you are going to take the shoes on and off, sew one side of a press stud in place on the strap and the other side on the shoe body. Alternatively, a few little invisible stitches can hold the strap in place.

HOW TO SEW LUNA'S

POLKA DOT DRESS

Luna woke up later than she had hoped, straightened her ears, fluffed up her tail and threw on her 'perfect for every occasion' dress, her 'no idea what else to wear' dress. She smiled – everyone should own a dress that makes them feel more like themselves.

Luna's *sewing* machine *winked*

at her from the corner of the room

and a day later Luna *slipped*

on her new **dress** and *twirled*

like she was *five* again

YOU WILL NEED

- Paper pattern for polka dot dress (see The Patterns)
- Fat quarter of 100% cotton fabric
- Scrap of contrast fabric for collar
- Two buttons
- Two press studs
- Bias binding, 2.5cm (1in) wide x 50cm (20in)
- Narrow ricrac, 50cm (20in)
- Basic sewing kit (see Materials)

Before you start, refer to The Patterns section for advice on using the patterns.

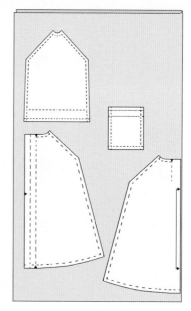

Fig.1

CUTTING OUT

1 Cut around your paper pattern pieces carefully. I cut on the black line, but to the outside not the inside.

2 Fold the fabric in half so that the right sides are together and short edges match. Pin your pattern pieces onto the fabric, using the layout as a guide (see **Fig.1**).

3 Cut the pieces out carefully. Mark any notches shown on the pattern as a solid triangle, with a *tiny* snip in the fabric to the centre of the triangle.

4 Cut the collar out of the contrast fabric.

TIP
To make cutting out more accurate, always iron your pattern and fabric to flatten out any creases before cutting.

MAKING UP

Making the Pockets:

1 Turn 0.5cm (¼in) on the top edge of the pocket to the wrong side and press. Turn 1cm (⅜in) to the right side of the fabric and pin the edges in place.

2 Sew 0.5cm (¼in) in on both edges as in **Fig.2**.

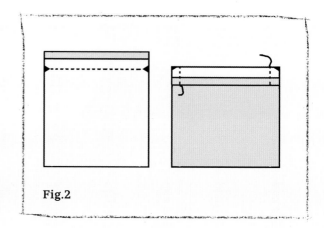

Fig.2

3 Trim the excess seam allowance away at the corners of the fold. Turn through, pushing out the corners with a knitting needle or similar tool. Turn and press the other edges of the pockets to the wrong side by 0.5cm (¼in) all the way around.

4 Lay ricrac across the right side top of the pocket, leaving 1cm (⅜in) overhang at the start and the finish. Sew a straight line through the centre of the ricrac to attach it to the pocket (**Fig.3**).

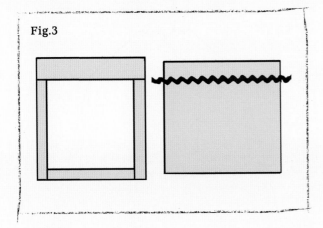

Fig.3

5 Position the pockets onto the front of the dress using your pattern as a guide, tucking the loose ricrac edge behind the pockets. Sew onto the dress front using an edgestitch (**Fig.4**).

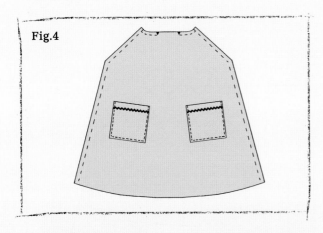

Fig.4

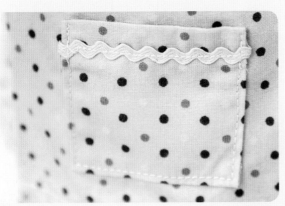

Making the Sleeves:

1 Fold the front in half, with the right sides together. Sew 1.5cm (⅝in) in from the folded edge for 4cm (1½in) to form the front pleat (**Fig.5**). On the wrong side press the pleat flat.

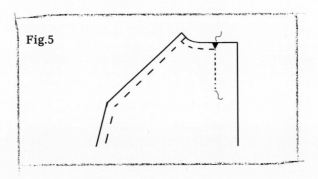

Fig.5

2 Press up the sleeve hems by 0.5cm (¼in) and then again by a further 1cm (⅜in). Edgestitch in place (**Fig.6**).

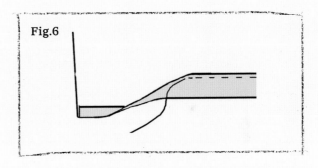

Fig.6

3 Flip to the right side and lay the ricrac over your stitching and sew a straight line through the centre of the ricrac to attach (**Fig.7**).

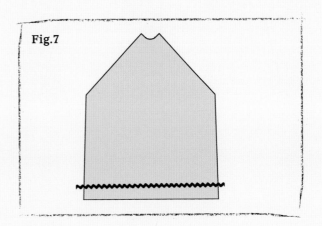

Fig.7

4 Use a zigzag stitch to finish the raw edges of the long back edge. With right sides together, pin the two back pieces together, and sew from the snip to the hem, with a 2cm (¾in) seam allowance (**Fig.8**).

6 With the right sides together, match one side of the front to one sleeve seam. Sew together with a 0.5cm (¼in) seam on each side. Repeat with the other side (**Fig.10**). Press the seams up towards the sleeve.

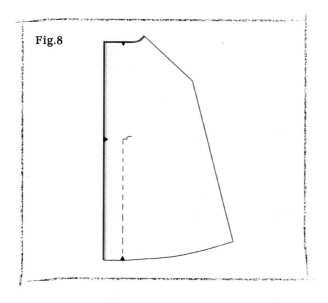

Fig.8

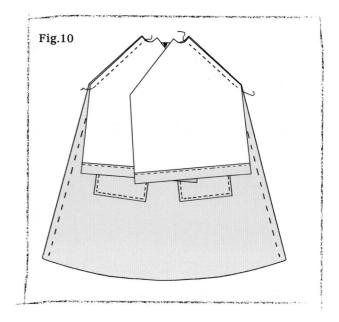

Fig.10

5 Press both the seam allowances to the right, all the way up to the snip at the neckline. On the left back press 1cm (⅜in) of the seam allowance back on itself as in **Fig.9**.

7 Join the back of the dress to the back of the sleeves at the shoulder seams in the same way (**Fig.11**).

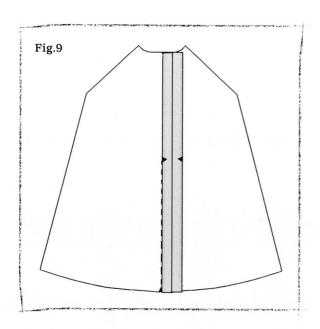

Fig.9

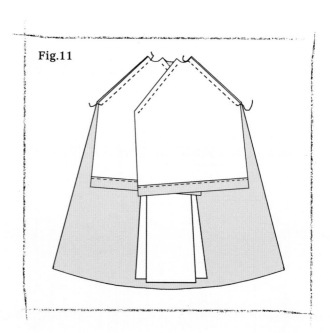

Fig.11

8 Press the seams up towards the sleeve and edgestitch along all the sleeve seams (**Fig.12**).

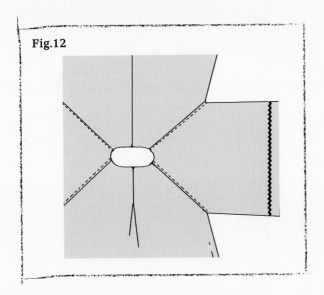

Fig.12

Making the Peter Pan Collar:

1 Take two collar pieces and with right sides together sew around the outside curve using a 0.5cm (¼in) seam allowance (**Fig.13**).

2 Trim off the excess seam allowance and turn through. Press flat ensuring the seam is to the edge. Repeat with the final two collar pieces.

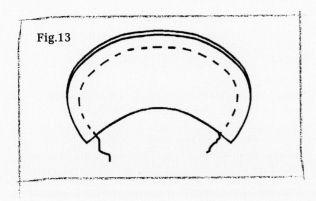

Fig.13

3 Pin the collars into position on the right side of the dress, matching up the edges and using the snips at the centre front and centre back to guide you. Note that your collars may cross slightly at the front as you are making them match 0.5cm (¼in) down from the centre front edge. Also note that your right-hand collar as worn will only go up to the snip and that the back will extend 1cm (⅜in) on as a facing (**Fig.14**).

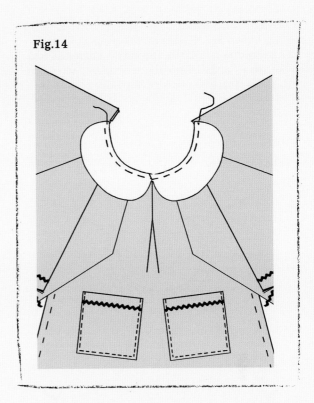

Fig.14

4 Staystitch or tack (baste) in place using a tiny seam allowance, slightly less than 0.5cm (¼in).

5 Trim the bias binding and cut it in half along the length, so you have a skinnier bias strip.

6 Leaving 0.5cm (¼in) overhang at each back edge (for turning under) and working with the wrong side of the bias facing upwards, match and pin the unpressed edge of the bias up to the edge of the neckline and sew 0.5cm (¼in) away from the neck edge (**Fig.15**).

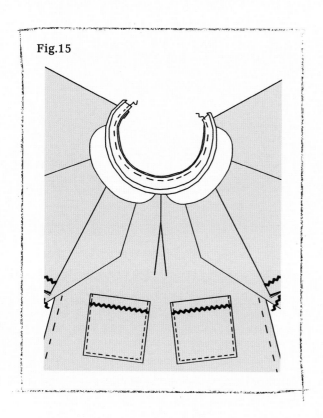

Fig.15

7 Trim the neck seam allowance to a scant 3mm (⅛in) and then fold the bias ends in and press the bias binding into the back of the neck edge to cover all the raw edges. Slipstitch the bias down to secure and finish the neckline. Remove the stay stitching if it is visible (**Fig.16**).

Fig.16

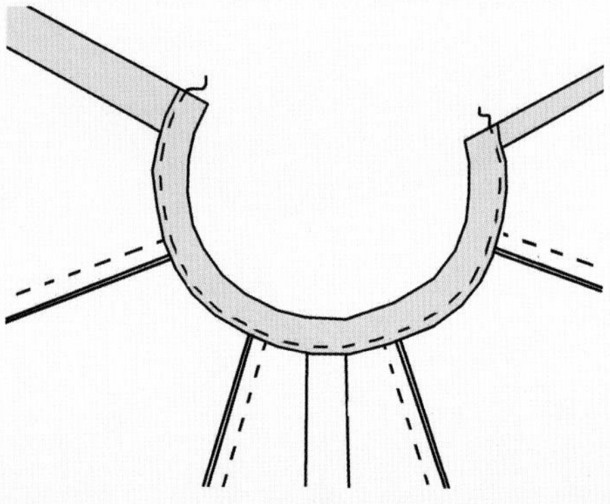

8 With the right sides together, match up the sleeve seams, underarm and side seams and pin in place. Sew 0.5cm (¼in) away from the edge as in **Fig.17**.

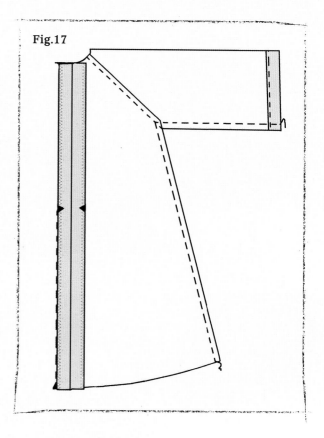

Fig.17

9 Press the seams towards the back of the dress as far as you can. Snip the fabric once at the underarm and turn the dress inside out.

Making the Hem:

1 Open up one folded edge of the bias binding. Working from the centre back seam, and with the right side of the bias binding facing the right side of the dress, turn in 0.5cm (¼in) on the bias binding short edge, line up the hem with the opened edge of the bias and sew in the valley fold of the bias – this will be 0.5cm (¼in) deep.

2 Stretch the bias slightly as you sew, to help you ease in the upper edge when you turn it at the next stage. Sew all the way around to the back seam.

3 Trim off the excess bias leaving 1cm (⅜in) to turn in. Press the bias flat to the wrong side of the dress, turning and pressing the end of the bias to meet the turned edge at the start (**Fig.18**).

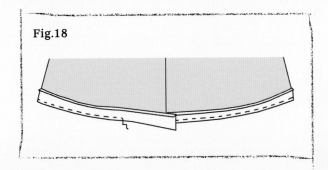

Fig.18

4 Secure the top edge of the bias, either by sewing through all the layers, making sure your sewing is parallel to the hem, or working with a slipstitch by hand.

FINISHING OFF

1 Sew the buttons in position at the back of the dress on the left-hand side – positioning one just under the collar and one 4cm (1½in) below. A press stud can be positioned below the button and sewn directly under, with the matching press stud component on the right-hand side of the dress facing outwards.

TIP
Use small 'doll' buttons, to keep in scale with the dress.

HOW TO SEW ALFIE'S

WAISTCOAT,
JEANS AND SHIRT

Expecting a rather lonely birthday away
from home for the first time, Luna
frowned at the knock on the front door.
Who could that be? To her utter delight
it was her brother Alfie, the best rabbit
she knew, who shared her love of clothes
and was always fun to be with.

Alfie gave his wool **waistcoat**

a quick pat with his **paw**,

straightening out the **check** of

his **cotton** shirt and noting with

satisfaction that he looked

very **dapper** in his new outfit

THE WAISTCOAT
YOU WILL NEED

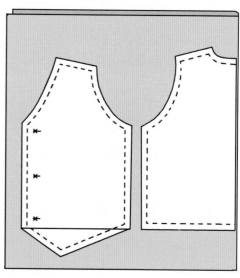

- Paper pattern for waistcoat (see The Patterns)
- Fine wool check, 20cm x 38cm (8in x 15in)
- Liberty cotton for lining, 20cm x 38cm (8in x 15in)
- Three buttons
- Three press studs (if not making buttonholes)
- Basic sewing kit (see Materials)

Before you start, refer to The Patterns section for advice on using the patterns.

Fig.1

CUTTING OUT

1 Cut around the paper pattern pieces carefully with scissors. I cut on the black line, to the outside not the inside.

2 Fold the fabric in half so that right sides are together. Try to make the fold fall on a main check line, so that your sides will mirror each other, and so the back has a main check line running through the centre back. Pin your pattern pieces onto the fabric, using **Fig.1** as a guide. Find a noticeable horizontal line in the check fabric and match the bottom edge of the back piece with the guideline given on the front pattern piece. Cut the pieces out carefully.

3 Unpin your pattern pieces and re-cut the pattern pieces in the Liberty fabric for the lining.

MAKING UP

1 Sew the fronts and back together as follows. Take the wool fabric pieces and with right sides together, match the shoulder seam of one front to one back shoulder seam. Sew together using a 0.5cm (¼in) seam allowance (**Fig.2**). Repeat with the other front and the remaining back shoulder seam (**Fig.3**). Press seams towards the back.

3 To make the front edges, with right sides together, match the edges of the lining up to the main pieces around the front edges and back neck. Pin in place and starting at one side front, sew around the edge using a 0.5cm (¼in) seam allowance, finishing at the other side front. To pivot at a corner, leave your needle down in the fabric, lift the presser foot and swing the fabric to line up with the new angle (**Fig.4**). Trim excess seam allowances where there are points, and snip into the seam allowance through the back neck to allow the seam allowance to sit flat once turned, but don't turn yet (**Fig.5**).

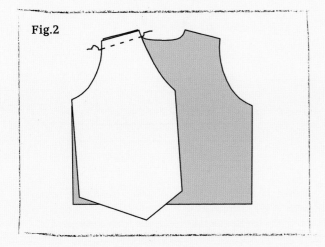

Fig.2

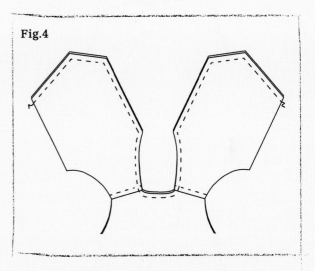

Fig.4

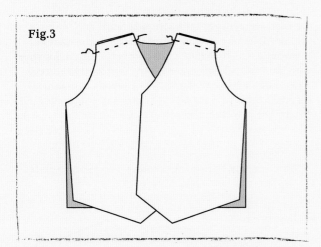

Fig.3

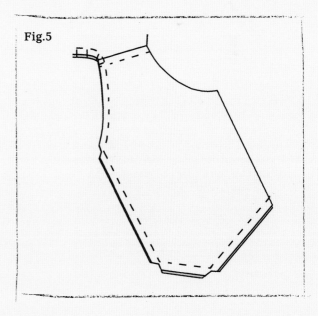

Fig.5

2 Take the lining fabric pieces and sew the shoulder seams as you did with the wool pieces.

4 Pin the lining to the main fabric around each armhole, matching the shoulder seams and edges. Sew each armhole using a 0.5cm (¼in) seam allowance (**Fig.6**). Snip into the seam allowance on the armholes to allow the seam allowance to sit flat once turned (**Fig.7**).

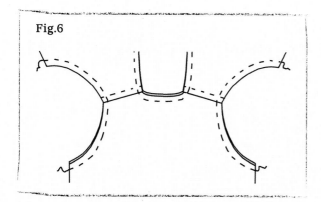

Fig.6

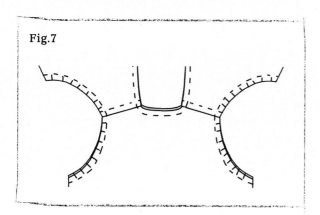

Fig.7

5 Push each front through the opening of the shoulder seam to the back, and turn through (**Fig.8**). Use a knitting needle or similar tool to push out the points and corners. Roll the edges between your fingers and thumb, to get the seams positioned on the edge, and then press the waistcoat front, neck edge and armholes flat.

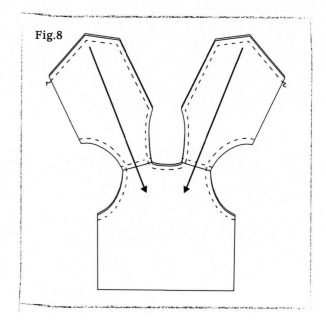

Fig.8

6 Take the front side edge and make sure that the lining/ outer edges are matching. Working one side at a time, bring the back outer fabric over the front outer, so that right sides are together. Match side seams. Bring the back lining over the front lining, so that it matches the front side seam on the lining side (**Fig.9**). The front piece will be enclosed between the back outer fabric and the back lining. Make sure that the top of the front side seam is tucked up tight to the back armhole seam. You will notice that the back side edges are 0.5cm (¼in) longer than the front – this is because the front has already had its hem turned up. Pin in place and using a 0.5cm (¼in) seam allowance, sew from the armhole down to the hem.

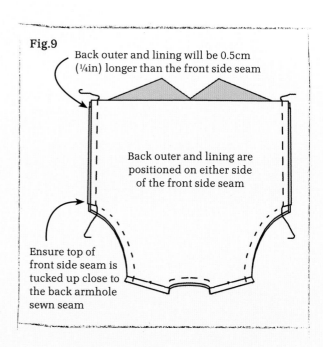

Fig.9

Back outer and lining will be 0.5cm (¼in) longer than the front side seam

Back outer and lining are positioned on either side of the front side seam

Ensure top of front side seam is tucked up close to the back armhole sewn seam

7 Turn the waistcoat out and press the side seam flat. Turn the back outer and lining hem edges up by 0.5cm (¼in) and slipstitch together to enclose the raw edges (**Fig.10**).

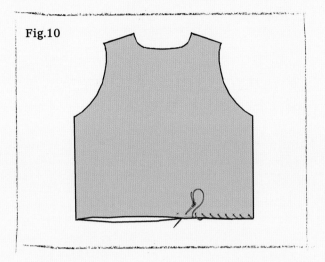

Fig.10

FINISHING OFF

1 If you are not confident with making buttonholes you can just sew on your buttons and use press studs to fasten. Both methods are given here.

If making buttonholes, mark the button and buttonhole positions on the waistcoat front using the pattern as a guide. Make buttonholes on the left-hand side (as worn). Cut through the buttonholes carefully using an unpicker and a pin at the far end of the buttonhole to ensure you don't rip any further than the buttonhole. Sew the buttons on the right-hand side (as worn) through both the front and the front facing.

If using buttons with press studs, sew the buttons on the left-hand side of the waistcoat (as worn) through both the front and the front facing. Position one side of a press stud under each button and sew in place. Sew the other half of each press stud onto the face of the right-hand side (as worn). The waistcoat is now ready for Alfie to try on.

TIP
If you are new to matching fabric checks, try photocopying your pattern onto clear acetate, so that you can see the design of the fabric through the clear pattern piece.

THE JEANS
YOU WILL NEED

- Paper pattern for jeans (see The Patterns)
- 100% lightweight cotton denim, 53cm x 38cm (21in x 15in)
- Elastic, 0.5cm (¼in) wide x 22cm (9in)
- One button
- Basic sewing kit (see Materials)

Before you start, refer to The Patterns section for advice on using the patterns.

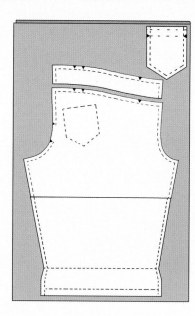

Fig.1

CUTTING OUT

1 Cut around your paper pattern pieces carefully using scissors. I cut on the black line, but to the outside not to the inside.

2 Join the upper leg and lower leg pattern pieces together *before* pinning or cutting. Fold the fabric in half so that right sides are together. Pin your pattern pieces onto the fabric, using **Fig.1** as a guide and cut out the pieces carefully. Mark any notches/triangles with a *tiny* snip in the fabric in the centre of the triangle.

MAKING UP

Making the Pockets:

1 Turn 0.5cm (¼in) on the top edge of the pocket to the wrong side and press. Turn 1cm (⅜in) to the right side of the fabric and pin the edges in place. Sew 0.5cm (¼in) in on both edges (**Fig.2**). Trim excess seam allowance away at the corners of the fold (**Fig.2**).

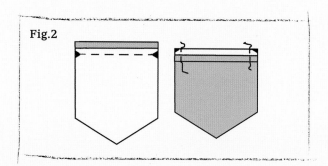

Fig.2

2 Turn through, pushing out the corners with a knitting needle. Turn and press the other edges of the pockets to the wrong side by 0.5cm (¼in) all the way around (**Fig.3**).

1 Make the hems by turning 0.5cm (¼in) to the wrong side and then a further 0.5cm (¼in) to enclose the raw edges (**Fig.6**). Press and then edgestitch in place.

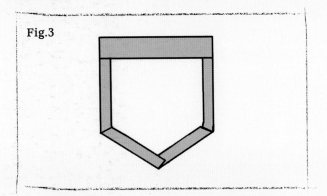

Fig.3

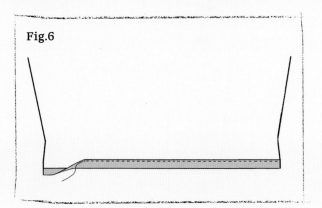

Fig.6

3 Topstitch the pocket as shown in **Fig.4**. Remember, when you need to turn a corner, leave your needle down in the fabric, lift the presser foot and turn. Now position the pockets onto the leg panels and sew in place using an edgestitch. Leave the top edge free (**Fig.5**).

2 Working one leg at a time, with right sides together, match the inside leg seams and sew with a 0.5cm (¼in) seam allowance (**Fig.7**). Repeat this with the other leg. Press the seams.

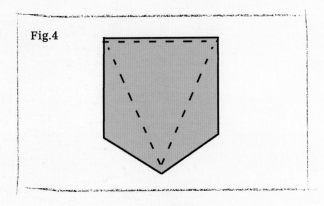

Fig.4

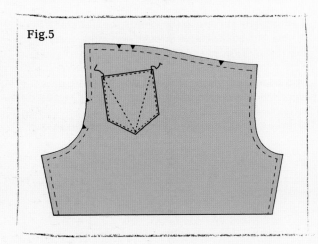

Fig.5

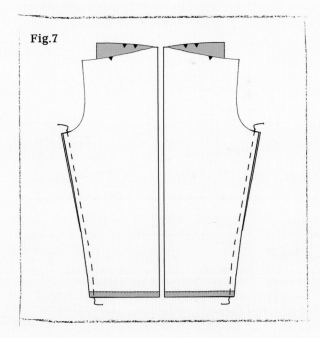

Fig.7

3 Turn one leg to be right side out and slide it, lower edge first, inside the other leg to sew the crotch. Matching edges and notches and inside leg seam, pin and sew the crotch with a 0.5cm (¼in) seam allowance, leaving an opening in the seam between the two notches for the tail (**Fig.8**).

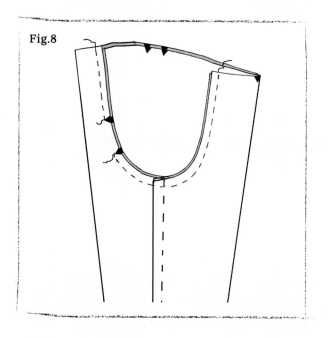

Fig.8

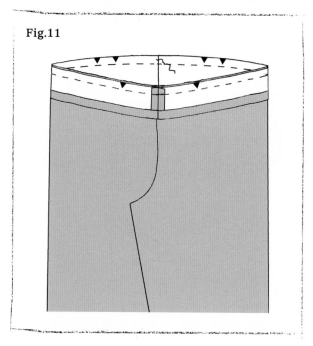

Fig.11

Making the Waist Facing and Waist:

1 With right sides together, join the short edges of the front facing with a 0.5cm (¼in) seam allowance and press open. With right sides together, join the short edges of the back facing with a 0.5cm (¼in) seam allowance and press open (**Fig.9**). Your facing will now be a circular loop. Press the lower edge of the facing (no notches) up to the wrong side by 0.5cm (¼in) all the way around (**Fig.10**).

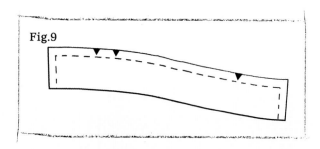

Fig.9

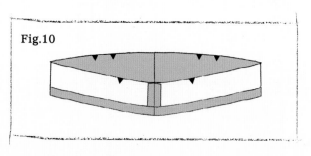

Fig.10

2 With right sides together, match up the edges of the waist to the facing using the notches and seams, and sew together using a 0.5cm (¼in) seam allowance (**Fig.11**).

3 For the casing, turn the facing to the inside, press and pin in place. Edgestitch around the top edge. Topstitch 1cm (⅜in) down from the top edge, starting at the centre back and finishing about 2.5cm (1in) away to leave an opening for threading the elastic (**Fig.12**).

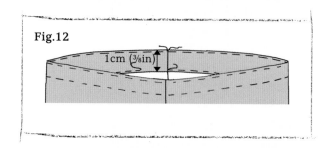

Fig.12

1cm (⅜in)

4 Put a safety pin through one end of the elastic and close the pin. Thread the elastic through the casing, ensuring that the unthreaded end of the elastic is still accessible. Adjust the gathering around the waist to be even and trim 2.5cm (1in) off the end of the elastic. Overlap the two elastic ends by 2.5cm (1in) and join using a zigzag machine stitch. Pull the waistband out so the joined ends of the elastic disappear into the casing. Close the casing opening with machine stitching.

5 If you wish, sew on a button to the left of the centre front seam. Finish by rolling up the bottoms of the jeans to create turn-ups.

THE SHIRT
YOU WILL NEED

- Paper pattern for shirt (see The Patterns)
- Fat quarter of 100% cotton gingham
- Six buttons
- Four press studs
- Basic sewing kit (see Materials)

Before you start, refer to The Patterns section for advice on using the patterns.

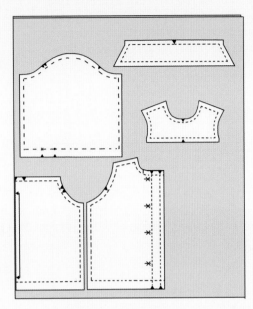

Fig.1

CUTTING OUT

1 Fold the fabric in half, right sides together. Try to ensure the horizontal check lines on the gingham run level, so when pinning you can match up the hem lines to a check line. Pin the pattern pieces onto the fabric using **Fig.1** as a guide and cut out all pieces. Mark any notches/triangles with a *tiny* snip in the fabric in the centre of the triangle.

MAKING UP

Making the Front Plackets:

1 Snip into both front pieces at the marked notch to a depth of 0.5cm (¼in). Press the short straight edge 0.5cm (¼in) to the wrong side up to the snip (**Fig.2**). Repeat with other side.

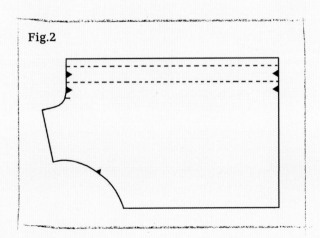

Fig.2

2 Turn the front long edge to the wrong side by 0.5cm (¼in) and press (**Fig.3**). Turn a further 1cm (⅜in) to the wrong side and press (**Fig.4**). Repeat with second side, ensuring it is facing the other way. Edgestitch down the front fold and the edge of the facing on both fronts (**Fig.5**).

Making the Back Yoke:

1 Use the notches in the back to create a box pleat, as follows. With the wrong side facing upwards bring the two notches to the centre back notch and pin. Tack (baste) in place 0.5cm (¼in) in from the edge (**Fig.6**). Press the pleat flat on the wrong side.

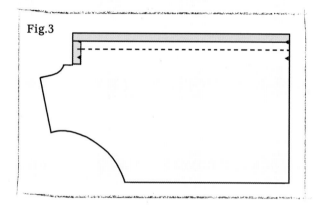

Fig.3

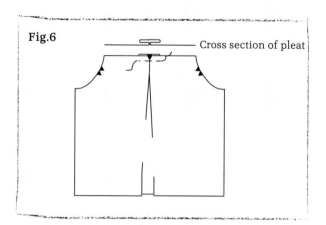

Fig.6

Cross section of pleat

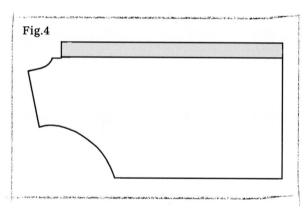

Fig.4

2 Lay the back panel with right side facing upwards. Put one yoke on the top with right sides downwards. Match up yoke seams and pin (**Fig.7**). Flip the back over to the wrong side (**Fig.8**). Match up the remaining yoke, and with the right side facing downwards, pin in place through all the layers (remember to remove the original pins) (**Fig.9**).

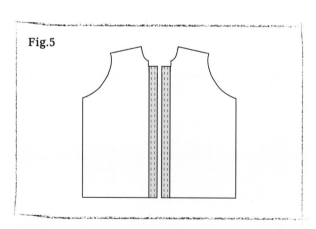

Fig.5

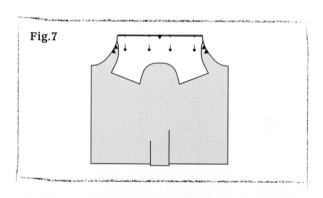

Fig.7

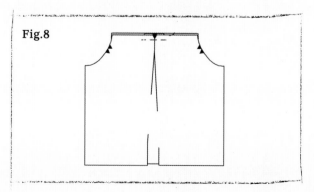

Fig.8

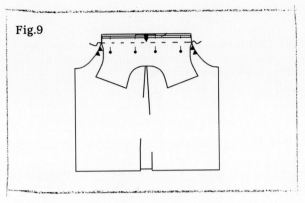

Fig.9

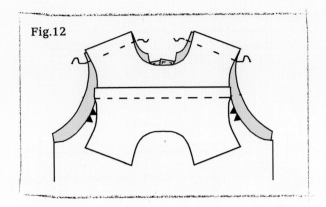

Fig.12

3 Sew all layers together using a 0.5cm (¼in) seam. Press the yokes back on themselves and then edgestitch the edge of the yoke through all layers (**Fig 10**).

2 Press the seams towards the yoke. Press 0.5cm (¼in) seam allowance of free yoke to the wrong side and then lay it over the already sewn yoke, matching the folded edges to the sewing line, and slipstitch in place (**Fig.13**). Flip to the right side and edgestitch the front yokes through all layers (**Fig.14**).

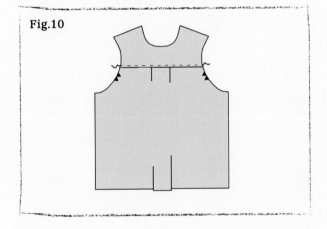

Fig.10

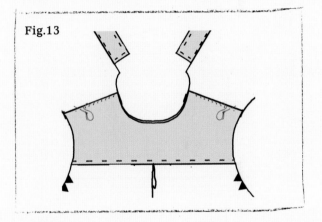

Fig.13

Making the Front Yoke:

1 Keeping the under yoke out of the way, take the front panels and match the front yoke seams to the front shoulders on each side. Pin in place and sew using 0.5cm (¼in) seam (**Fig.11**). The back will look like **Fig.12**.

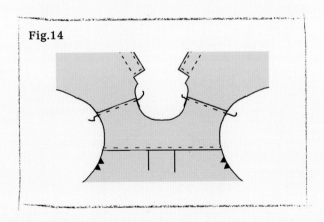

Fig.14

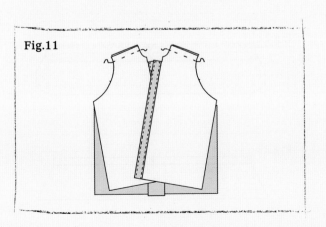

Fig.11

Sewing the Sleeve Hems:

1 Hem the sleeves by turning 0.5cm (¼in) to the wrong side and then a further 0.5cm (¼in). Press and then edgestitch through all layers (**Fig.15**).

Fig.15

2 Use the pattern piece to mark the pleat positions. With the wrong side facing upwards bring the X to match the dot. Press and pin (**Fig.16**). Repeat with other sleeve, which will be a mirror image. Flip to be right side up and hand sew a button in place through the pleat layers to hold in place.

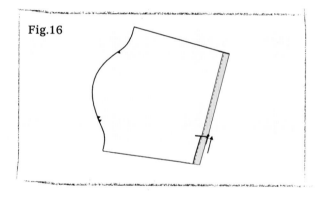

Fig.16

3 With right sides together, match one sleeve to the armhole using the notches to position. Pin in place and sew together with a 0.5cm (¼in) seam (**Fig.17**). Repeat with the other sleeve and armhole. Press the seams towards the sleeve.

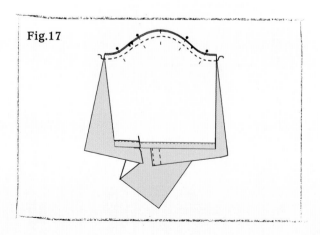

Fig.17

Making the Collar:

1 Staystitch 0.5cm (¼in) in from the edge of the neck, using a long stitch that can easily be removed. Snip into the fabric where the curves are tight on the neck but don't cut past the staystitching (**Fig.18**).

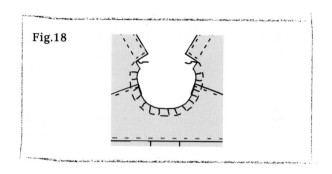

Fig.18

2 Take one collar piece and press the notched edge to the wrong side by 0.5cm (¼in) (**Fig.19**). With right sides together, pin the two collar pieces together, matching the corners, and sew along the two short ends and the long un-notched edge with a 0.5cm (¼in) seam. Note the pressed edge of one collar will mean it doesn't match up along the notched edge – see **Fig.20**. Trim the corners to reduce the bulk (**Fig.21**). Turn the collar out and push the corners out using a knitting needle or similar tool (**Fig.22**).

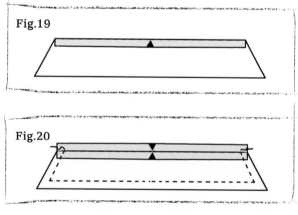

Fig.19

Fig.20

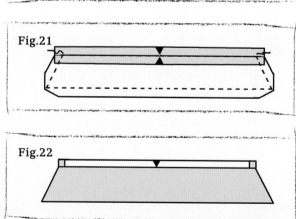

Fig.21

Fig.22

3 Pin the unturned collar piece into positon on the right side of the shirt, using the centre back snip to guide you. The end of the collar will match with the notches in the front panel. Staystitch or tack (baste) in place using a tiny seam allowance (slightly less than 0.5cm/¼in). Sew with a 0.5cm (¼in) seam allowance – you will need the snips in the neck edge to give the ease to enable you to sew in the collar strip (**Fig.23**).

FINISHING OFF

1 With right sides together, match up the sleeve seams, underarm and side seams and pin in place. Sew 0.5cm (¼in) away from the edge (**Fig.26**). Press the seams towards the back of the shirt as far as you can. Turn the shirt inside out.

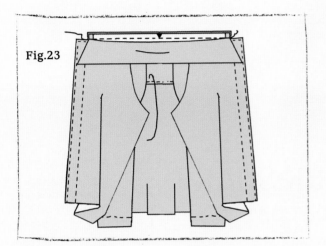

Fig.23

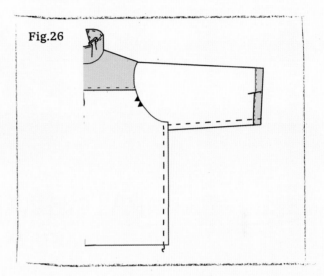

Fig.26

4 Using an iron, press the seam allowance away from the shirt and up towards the collar. Bring the free collar edge down to match your sewing line and enclose all the raw edges. Slipstitch the edge of the collar onto the line of stitching (**Fig.24**). Remove stay stitching if it is visible and then edgestitch around the collar (**Fig.25**).

2 Hem the shirt by turning 0.5cm (¼in) to the wrong side and then a further 0.5cm (¼in). Press and edgestitch through all layers.

3 Make the buttonholes and sew on the buttons (or use press studs instead) in the same way as the waistcoat – see The Waistcoat, Finishing Off, step 1. Now dress Alfie in his outfit and see how wonderful he looks!

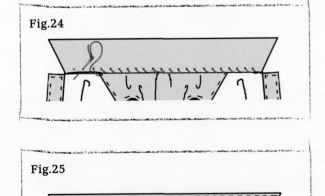

Fig.24

Fig.25

HOW TO SEW LUNA'S

PATCHWORK SCARF
AND WOOL COAT

Luna's favourite thing was her lovely
patchwork scarf. Her grandma had given
it to her for her birthday two years ago
and Luna was sure that it brought her
luck. Today she needed luck as it was
her first day in the big city, hoping to
impress at a job interview.

Noisy **cities** aren't nice for rabbit ears, but **Luna** was an illustrator, and **illustrators** had to work in cities for a while. She took a **deep** breath, **snuggling** her lucky **scarf** around her neck...

THE SCARF
YOU WILL NEED

- Paper triangle pattern for patchwork scarf (see The Patterns)
- Assorted scraps of Liberty fabrics, 6.5cm (2½in) square minimum
- Basic sewing kit (see Materials)

Before you start, refer to The Patterns section for advice on using the patterns.

CUTTING OUT

1 Use the triangle pattern to cut sixty-four triangles from your assorted fabrics. Lay out your fabric pieces to decide on the order you would like, arranging the triangles in two rows, with thirty-two triangles in each row (**Fig.1**). Placing light and dark pieces alternately works well. When you are happy with the order of the pieces, stack the triangles in two separate piles, one for each row.

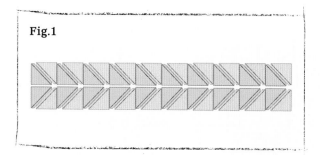

Fig.1

MAKING UP

1 Sew the patchwork triangles together, using a 0.5cm (¼in) seam allowance throughout the making of the scarf. Start by taking two triangles from the first pile, pin them right sides together and sew along the long diagonal side (**Fig.2**). Press the seam open to form a square unit (**Fig.3**). Repeat this with all of the triangles in this row. Repeat this to sew the triangles of the second row together.

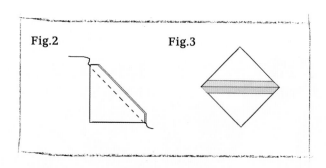

Fig.2   Fig.3

2 Sew the square units together as follows. Pin two square units right sides together and sew them together along one edge (**Fig.4**). Add the next square unit in the same way and continue until you have sewn the first row together. Press the seams open (**Fig.5**). Sew the second row in the same way. If you have a rotary cutter you could straighten up the long edges in case any edges are slightly out.

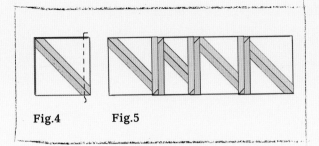

Fig.4   Fig.5

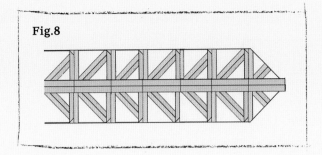

Fig.8

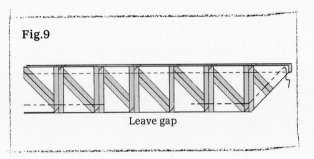

Fig.9

Leave gap

3 Both ends of each row will now need trimming to a diagonal, to give a point at each end of the scarf. It may be that one end will follow the triangular shape (in which case unpick the last triangle on the two strips and discard it), but the other end will need to be cut across two joined pieces. Cut 0.5cm (¼in) below the corner point of the square to allow for a seam allowance, as shown in **Fig.6**.

5 Trim excess seam allowance away from the points and then turn through, using a knitting needle or similar tool to push out the corners. Roll the seams out to the edges using your fingers and then press flat. Turn in the seam allowance along the gap and slipstitch closed. The scarf is now ready to bring Luna some luck!

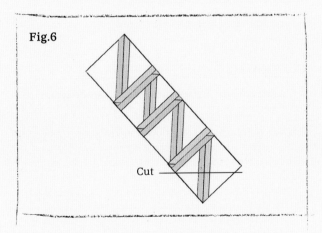

Fig.6

Cut

4 Place the two rows right sides together, matching seams, and sew along one long edge with 0.5cm (¼in) seam allowance (**Fig.7**). Press the seam open (**Fig.8**). Fold the scarf right sides together along the length again and pin all the other edges together. Sew along the edges, including the triangle point, leaving a gap of about three squares along the long edge to allow the scarf to be turned through (**Fig.9**).

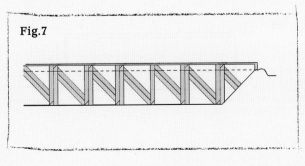

Fig.7

THE WOOL COAT
YOU WILL NEED

- Paper pattern for coat (see The Patterns)
- Wool felt, 28cm x 91.5cm (11in x 36in)
- Eight buttons
- Bias binding, 2.5cm (1in) wide x 50cm (20in)
- Basic sewing kit (see Materials)

Before you start, refer to The Patterns section for advice on using the patterns.

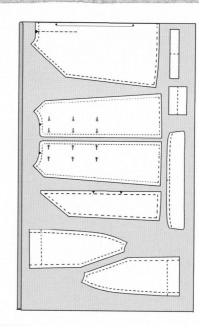

Fig.1

CUTTING OUT

1 Cut around your paper pattern pieces carefully. I cut on the black line, but to the outside not the inside.

2 When working with felt it does not have a wrong side or right side but a shaded right side is shown on diagrams as a visual aid for the instructions. Begin by folding the felt in half with the short edges matching. Pin the pattern pieces onto the fabric, using the layout in **Fig.1** as a guide. Cut the pieces out carefully. Mark any notches/triangles with a *tiny* snip in the fabric into the centre of the triangle.

MAKING UP

Making the Mock Pockets:

1 Fold the pocket piece in half, so long edges are together, and press with an iron (**Fig.2**). Position the piece onto the side panel between the snips, with the folded edge away from the seam. Edgestitch 2mm (1/16in) in from the edge along both short edges. Repeat with other side (**Fig.3**).

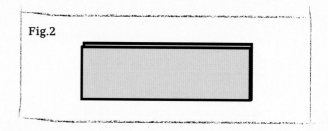

Fig.2

Fig.3

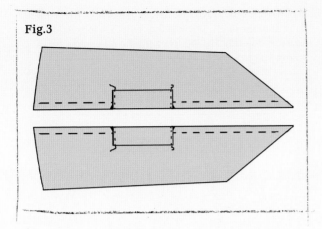

2 With right sides together, match the side panel to the front panel and sew with a 0.5cm (¼in) seam allowance. Press the seam allowance towards the front panel (**Fig.4**). Edgestitch 2mm (¹⁄₁₆in) away from the seam, along the seam on the front panel. Repeat this step with other side panel and front panel (**Fig.5**).

Fig.4

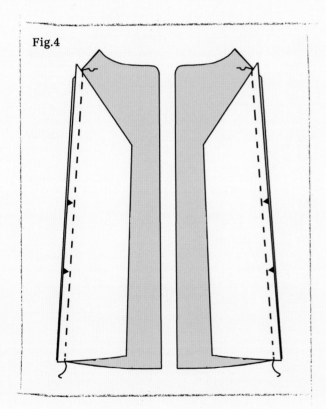

Fig.5

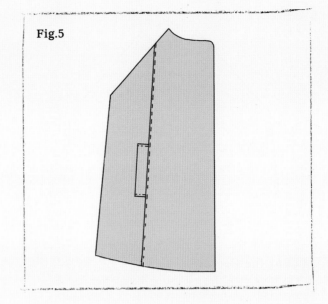

3 Fold the back in half and sew 1.5cm (⅝in) in from the fold for 7cm (2¾in) (**Fig.6**). Press the pleat flat and open on the wrong side. On the right side, topstitch 0.5cm (¼in) in to hold it down, pivoting with a triangular end as in **Fig.7** to topstitch up the other side.

Fig.6

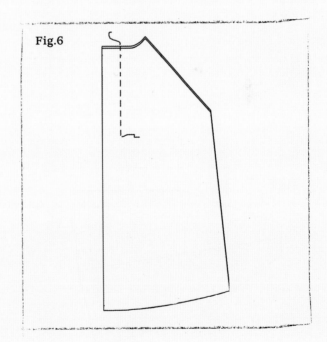

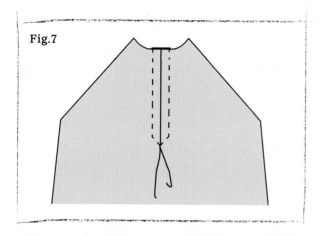

Fig.7

2 With right sides together, match one side of the front to one shoulder seam. Sew together with a 0.5cm (¼in) seam on each side (**Fig.10**). Repeat with the other side. Press seams up towards the sleeve.

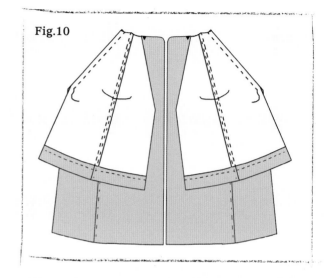

Fig.10

Making the Sleeves:

1 Take two sleeve pieces and sew them together with a 0.5cm (¼in) seam allowance along the curved seam (**Fig.8**). Press the seam allowance to one side (it will be the back) and edgestitch along the shoulder seam on the back panel. Ensure the seam allowances of the two sleeves are pressed towards opposite sides to get a left and a right sleeve. Turn and press the sleeve hems up by 1.5cm (⅝in) and sew 1cm (⅜in) up from the hem fold (**Fig.9**).

3 Join the back of the coat to the back of the sleeves at the shoulder seams in the same manner (**Fig.11**). Press the seams up towards the sleeve. Edgestitch 2mm (¹⁄₁₆in) in from the edge along all of the sleeve seams (**Fig.12**).

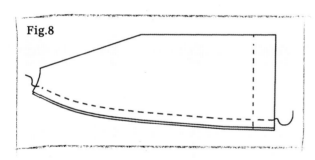

Fig.8

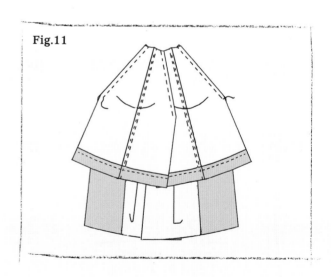

Fig.11

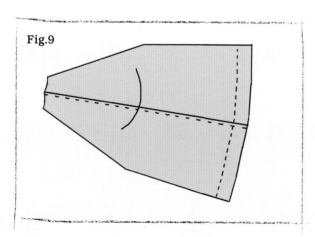

Fig.9

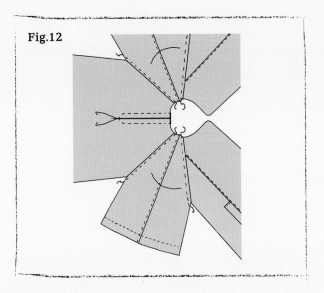

Fig.12

Making the Collar:

1 Match the two collar pieces and sew around the outside using an edgestitch 2mm (1/16in) in from the edge (**Fig.13**). Pin the collar into positon on the right side of the coat, using the centre back snip to guide you. The end of the collar will match with the notches in the front panel (**Fig.14**). Staystitch or tack (baste) in place using a tiny seam allowance (slightly less than 0.5cm/1/4in).

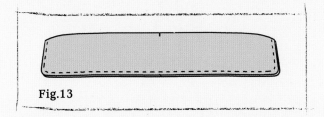

Fig.13

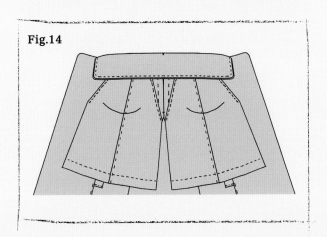

Fig.14

2 Match the front facing pieces up with the front, covering the front panel and part of the collar, and pin in place (**Fig.15**). Trim down a 19cm (7½in) piece of the bias binding by cutting through the centre lengthways.

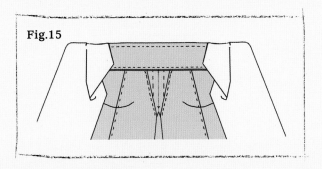

Fig.15

3 Take the unfolded edge of the bias and place it so it overlaps the front facing by 1cm (3/8in) and matches up with the back neck edge. It should finish with the other end overlapping with the other front facing by 1cm (3/8in) (**Fig.16**). Trim any excess length from the bias strip.

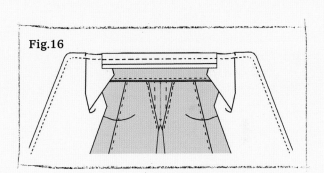

Fig.16

4 Using a 0.5cm (1/4in) seam allowance, sew 0.5cm (1/4in) up from the hem, up on one front edge, around the soft corner, across the collar and, turning a soft corner, come back down the other front edge. Stop 0.5cm (1/4in) before the end. Trim off excess fabric from the corners and the neckline, cutting to 3mm (1/8in) from the stitching line.

5 On the wrong side, make sure the bias ends are under the front facings and press the binding into the back of the neck edge to cover all raw edges (**Fig.17**). Slipstitch the binding in place, to secure and finish the neckline. Remove stay stitching if it's visible.

2 Position a sleeve tab onto the front sleeve, lining up the edgestitching with the hem stitching. Stay stitch in place. Position a button 0.5cm (¼in) in from the end of the tab and sew it in place using double thread. Repeat with the other sleeve, making sure it is an 'opposite' to the first sleeve (**Fig.19**).

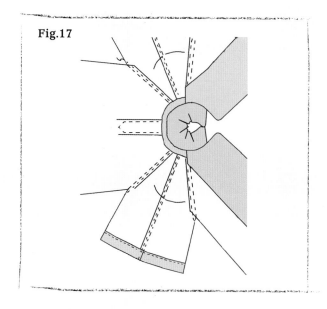

Fig.17

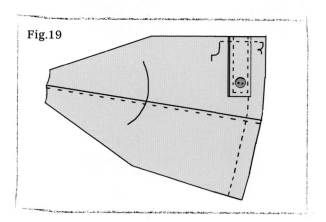

Fig.19

Finishing the Sleeves:

1 Fold the sleeve tabs so that the short edges match. Edgestitch around three sides (**Fig.18**).

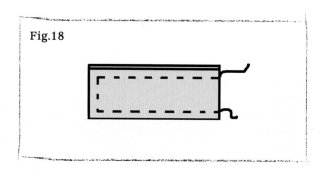

Fig.18

3 With right sides together, match up the sleeve seams, underarm and side seams and pin in place. Sew 0.5cm (¼in) away from the edge (**Fig.20**). Press seams towards the back of the coat as far as you can. Snip the fabric once at the underarm and then turn the coat inside out.

2 Trim off the excess fabric from the corners and then turn right sides out. Push the front corners out gently and press flat. Press the bias up to the wrong side of the coat, tucking the raw edge of the end of the binding under the front facing panels (**Fig.22**). Secure the top edge of the binding with a hand slipstitch.

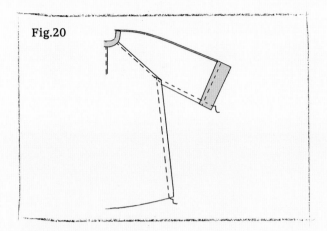

Fig.20

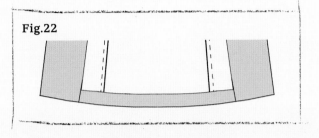

Fig.22

Completing the Hem:

1 To make the hem, with right sides together, pin together the lower edge of the front to the front facing. Open up one folded edge of the remaining full-width bias binding. With the right side of the binding facing the right side, overlap the binding 1cm (⅜in) over the front facing, line up the opened edge of the binding to the hem and pin all round to the other front facing, leaving an overlap of 1cm (⅜in) (**Fig.21**). Now sew from the front edge, along to the binding and sew in the valley fold of the bias – this will be 0.5cm (¼in) deep. Sew all the way around to the corner of the other front edge.

TIP
The method of binding hems used for this project is really easy and effective for circular skirt hems on your own garments.

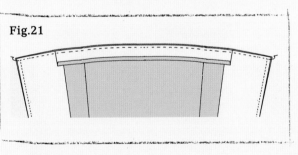

Fig.21

3 After pressing all edges, edgestitch from the raglan front sleeve seam around the front of the coat, along the hem edge and then back up the other front edge to finish at the other raglan front sleeve seam (**Fig.23**).

FINISHING OFF

1 Mark the button and buttonhole positions on the coat front using the pattern as a guide. Make buttonholes on the right-hand side (as worn), ensuring the facing is lying in the correct position behind the front (see Tip). Cut through buttonholes carefully using an unpicker and a pin at the far end of the buttonhole to ensure you don't rip any further than the buttonhole.

2 To finish, sew the buttons on the left-hand side of the coat (as worn) through both the front and the front facing. Luna's warm coat is now ready to wear!

Fig.23

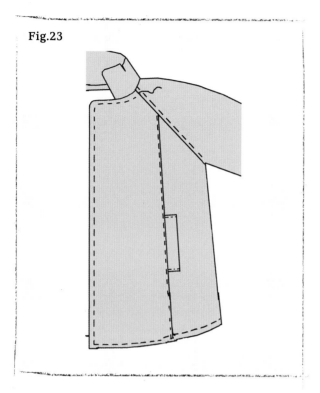

TIP
If you are not confident with making buttonholes please practise on some scrap felt. It would be a shame to spoil the coat after all your hard work.

HOW TO SEW LUNA'S

TWEED BAG,
TWEED SKIRT AND BOOTS

Luna hugged herself gleefully as she read the invitation to the La Clairière Christmas party – a new outfit was a must! The next day she put on her best winter shopping clothes, a lace top, beautiful tweed A-line skirt and matching bag just the right size for newly found treasures.

The *tweed* fabric was beautiful, woven together with **perfect pastels** that danced and dipped through a **blue** as **pretty** as a winter **sky**

THE TWEED BAG
YOU WILL NEED

- Paper pattern for tweed bag
  (see The Patterns)
- 100% wool tweed for bag and skirt,
  23cm x 48cm (9in x 19in)
- 100% cotton lining fabric, 10cm x 28cm
  (4in x 11in)
- One wooden button
- One press stud
- Grosgrain ribbon, 0.5cm (¼in) wide
  x 38cm (15in)
- Stranded embroidery cotton (floss)
- Basic sewing kit (see Materials)

Before you start, refer to The Patterns section
for advice on using the patterns.

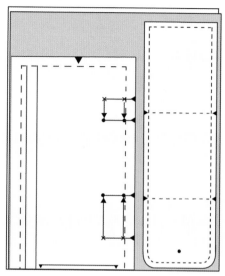

Fig.1

CUTTING OUT

1 Cut around your paper pattern piece carefully. I cut
on the black line, but to the outside not the inside. Seam
allowances are included.

2 Pin the pattern piece onto the fabric, using the layout
shown in **Fig.1** as a guide. Note that both the bag and the
skirt are shown on the diagram but the bag should be cut
out of single-thickness fabric. Cut out the pieces. Mark
any notches/triangles with a *tiny* snip in the fabric. Unpin
the pattern pieces from the cut fabric. Pin the bag pattern
piece onto the lining, cut out and prepare as above. These
fabrics have a right and a wrong side (shown in the
illustrations and referred to in the instructions).

MAKING UP

1 With right sides together match and pin the bag's tweed
flap end to the lining flap end, matching notches. Sew
using a 0.5cm (¼in) seam allowance, from the level of one
notch around one curved corner along the flap edge and
around the other curved corner to the level of the next
notch (**Fig.2**). With right sides together, match the other
end of the long pieces and sew along this edge (**Fig.3**).
Press the seam allowance open and flat.

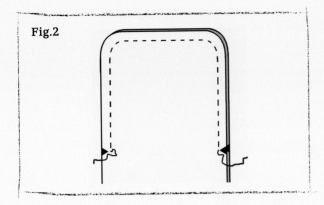

Fig.2

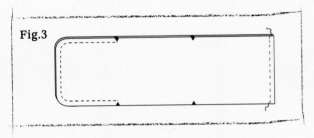

Fig.3

3 To sew the lining body, repeat step 2 above. Repeat with the other side. Move the flap out of the way and sew one side with a 0.5cm (¼in) seam allowance, stopping where your previous sewing finished (**Fig.6**). Sew the other side in the same way but leave an opening of at least 3.5cm (1⅜in) to be able to turn everything through.

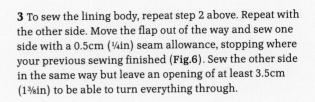

Fig.6

2 To sew the main body of the bag, find the notch that is halfway down the free edge of the tweed – this is the fold point, and the eventual bottom of the bag. Match the edges of the tweed piece together and pin – you should be looking to match the notch where the flap finishes to the seam line of the other end. Repeat with the other side (**Fig.4**). Sew each side with a 0.5cm (¼in) seam allowance, keeping the flap out of the way (**Fig.5**).

4 Create a T-shaped bottom in the outer fabric and in the lining as follows. Working with one corner at a time, flatten the corners so the side seam lines up with the bottom fold. You can judge this by pushing a pin through the seam and making sure it comes out on the bottom foldline. Draw a guideline at right angles 1.5cm (⅝in) from the sewn point. Sew across the drawn guideline (**Fig.7**). Cut off the excess seam allowance to within 3mm (⅛in) of the stitching line (**Fig.8**). Turn the little bag inside out, pushing out the corners. Roll the seam edges to the outside between your fingers and gently press the flap flat using an iron.

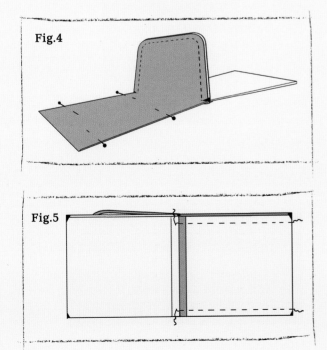

Fig.4

Fig.5

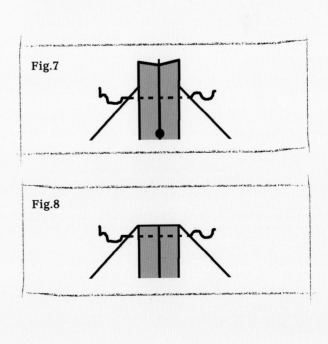

Fig.7

Fig.8

5 Sew up the lining opening by pulling the lining bag out of the bag and, making sure the seam allowance is tucked inside the opening, slipstitch the opening closed. Now push the lining into the main body of the bag and finger press the front edge of the bag down.

FINISHING OFF

1 Using all six strands of the embroidery thread, sew around the bag flap using a running stitch about 0.5cm (¼in) in from the edge (**Fig.9**). Mark the button position on the flap if you haven't already done so, and then sew the button on with several strands of embroidery thread.

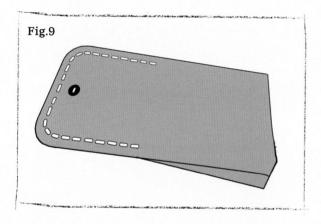

Fig.9

2 Fold the flap over the bag and push a pin through the button to find and mark the press stud positions on the flap and the main body of the bag. Sew on the two components of the press stud – the female side on the under flap and the male side on the main body of the bag.

3 Fold the ribbon back 1cm (⅜in) at each end. Pin the ribbon ends to the sides of the bag's front edge so the folded ribbon ends are facing the bag lining (**Fig.10**). Make sure there is no twist in the ribbon. Hand sew in place inside the bag on each side to finish. The bag is now ready for Luna's shopping trip.

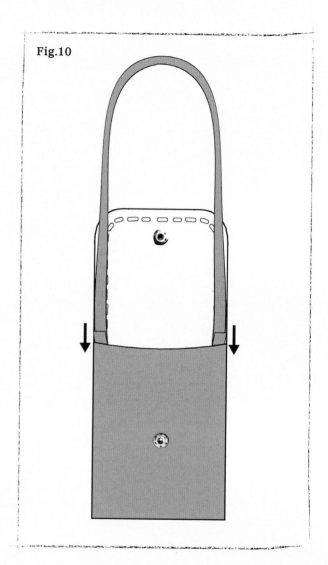

Fig.10

TIP
The shape and techniques used to make this tiny bag could easily be scaled up to make a person-sized messenger bag. The T-shaped bottom makes the bag more voluminous and useful.

THE TWEED SKIRT
YOU WILL NEED

- Paper pattern for tweed skirt (see The Patterns)
- 100% wool tweed – see Tweed Bag
- Grosgrain ribbon, 1.5cm (⅝in) wide x 40cm (16in)
- One wooden button
- One press stud
- Basic sewing kit (see Materials)

Before you start, refer to The Patterns section for advice on using the patterns.

CUTTING OUT

1 Cut around your paper pattern piece carefully. I cut on the black line, but to the outside not the inside. Seam allowances are included.

2 Pin the pattern piece onto the fabric, as described on the pattern, and cut out. Mark the notches shown on the pattern with either a *tiny* snip in the fabric or with a water-soluble pen or chalk marker. Unpin your pattern pieces from the cut fabric. Mark the embroidery position with a water-soluble pen or chalk marker later on if you wish. These fabrics have a right and a wrong side (shown in the illustrations and referred to in the instructions).

MAKING UP

1 To make the front pleats lay the skirt out with right side facing up. Find the A notches and crosses and match up to the B notches and spots, making the excess fabric lay behind notch A (**Fig.1**). Press excess fabric towards the centre front (**Fig.2**).

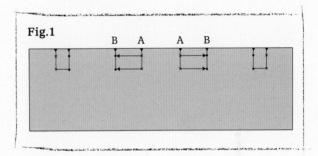

Fig.1

B A   A B

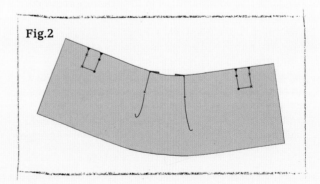

Fig.2

2 To make the back pleats, using your notches as guides, find the C notches and crosses and match up to the D notches and spots, making the excess fabric lay behind notch C (**Fig.3**). Press excess fabric towards the back edge. Sew down all pleats with an edgestitch (**Fig.4**).

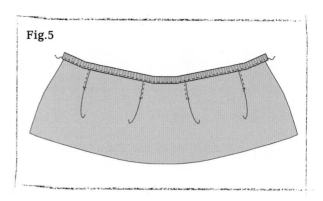

Fig.5

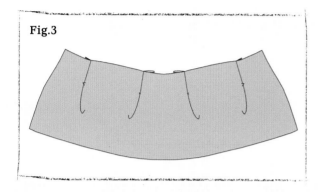

Fig.3

4 With right sides together, match the back edges of the skirt and sew from below the notch down to the hem edge using a 1cm (⅜in) seam allowance (**Fig.6**).

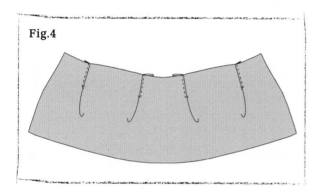

Fig.4

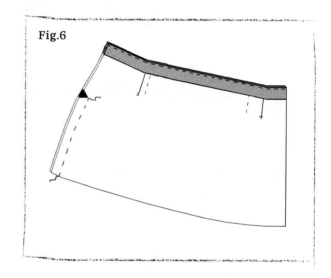

Fig.6

3 To make the waist facing, with the right side of the skirt facing upwards, take the ribbon and lay it so that the lower edge is 1cm (⅜in) down from the top edge of the skirt. The ribbon will extend past the top edge by 0.5cm (¼in). There should also be a little bit of extra ribbon extending over the back edges on each side. Pin in place, and tack (baste) too if you wish, and then edgestitch the ribbon onto the tweed (**Fig.5**). Trim the excess ribbon from the ends so it is in line with the skirt edges. Fold the ribbon to the wrong side of the skirt and press the top edge.

TIP
This skirt would look stylish in needlecord or denim fabric. You could add a ruffle, lace or velvet ribbon to the hem instead of embroidery.

5 To finish the skirt opening, press the seam allowance open, pressing the 1cm (⅜in) seam allowance back above the notch as well. Turn the skirt to be right side out. Turn the ribbon edges in, so the foldline matches that of the skirt, and edgestitch around the skirt opening (**Fig.7**).

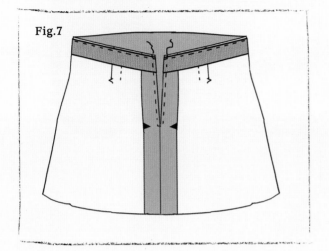

Fig.7

FINISHING OFF

1 Your Luna's waist may be a different size depending on how you've stuffed her, so try the skirt on to decide how much the skirt needs to overlap at the back. When you have done this, mark the press stud positions and sew on the two components of the press stud – the female side on the left-hand side (as worn) and the male side on the right-hand side (**Fig.8**). If you wish to have a decorative button on the skirt sew it on the left-hand side (as worn).

2 Press up a 1cm (⅜in) hem allowance to the wrong side of the skirt and tack (baste) it in place. If you need to mark some guidelines for the embroidery do so now – the stitches should be about 1cm (⅜in) wide and the lower edge should be 0.5cm (¼in) up from the folded edge. Work a herringbone stitch around the hem using six strands of embroidery thread (see Techniques: Hand Sewing Stitches: Herringbone Stitch). Luna's tweed skirt is now ready to wear.

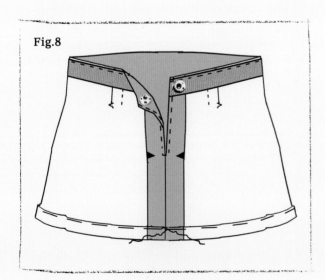

Fig.8

THE BUNNY BOOTS
YOU WILL NEED

- Paper pattern for boots (see The Patterns)
- Wool felt, 11.5cm x 41cm (4½in x 16in)
- Stranded embroidery cotton (floss)
- Basic sewing kit (see Materials)

Before you start, refer to The Patterns section for advice on using the patterns.

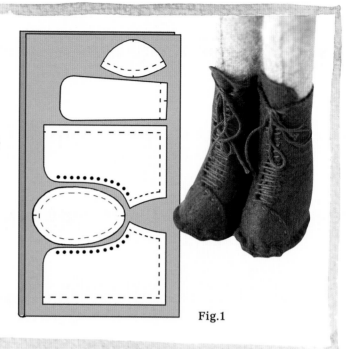

Fig.1

CUTTING OUT

1 Cut around your paper pattern pieces carefully. I cut on the black line, but to the outside not the inside. Seam allowances are included.

2 Pin the pattern pieces onto the fabric, using the layout in **Fig.1** as a guide. Cut out the pieces. Mark the notches shown on the pattern with either a *tiny* snip in the fabric or using a water-soluble pen or chalk. Mark the lacing positions with a water-soluble pen or chalk. Unpin the patterns from the fabric.

MAKING UP

1 The edges of the felt do not need finishing as it does not fray. There is no definite right or wrong side to felt, but I have referred to 'right' and 'wrong' to help you sew. These instructions describe making one boot at a time – you could work this way or repeat each step and make up both boots together.

2 To make the toe cap and sides, position one side piece so that 0.5cm (¼in) is sitting under the toe cap. Pin into place and then position the other side in the same way on the toe cap. For clarity, this is shown in **Fig.2** as though the felt is transparent.

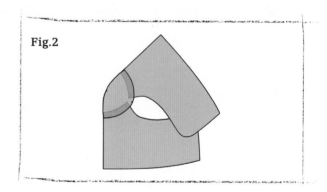

Fig.2

3 To add the tongue, position the tongue piece so that the centre sits in line with the centre of the toe cap and so 0.5cm (¼in) is sitting under the toe cap and sides (**Fig.3**). Pin in place and then tack (baste) all layers into position.

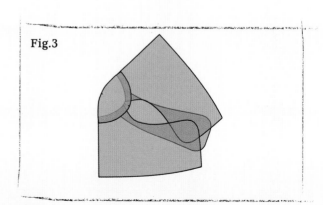

Fig.3

4 To stitch the toe cap, use six strands of embroidery thread and sew through the cap and other layers using a running stitch 3mm (⅛in) from the curved edge (**Fig.4**). Remove tacking (basting) threads.

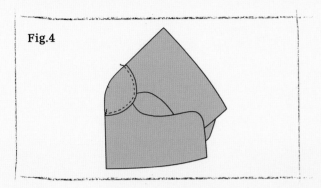

Fig.4

5 To sew the back seam, turn the boot so right sides are together and the two long back edges match. Sew together using a 0.5cm (¼in) seam allowance and a backstitch with two strands of embroidery thread (**Fig.5**).

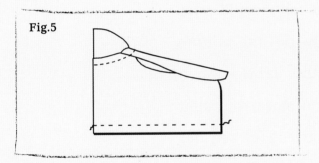

Fig.5

6 To attach the boot to the sole, with wrong sides together, match the notches at the front of the toe cap to the sole, and the back seam to the other sole notch. Now tack (baste) the sole onto the boot, easing the felt in place as necessary (**Fig.6**). Using six strands of embroidery thread, sew the boot to the sole using a neat running stitch about 3mm (⅛in) from the curved edge (**Fig.7**). Remove any tacking (basting) threads.

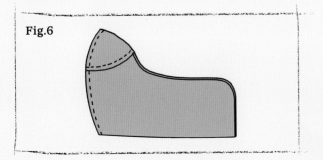

Fig.6

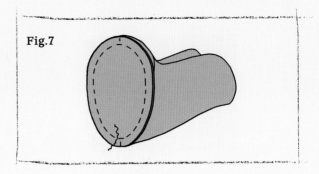

Fig.7

Adding the Lacing:

1 To add the lacing, mark the lacing holes on the boot sides if you haven't already done so (**Fig.8**). You may find it easier to do this stage with the boot on your rabbit's leg. Slip the boot on and position the sides of the boot and the tongue into the right position and if you wish, pin into the leg (ouch!).

2 Take a metre (yard) long piece of embroidery thread (all six strands) and start at the bottom by sewing up through the left-hand side of the boot (as worn), from the back of the piece through to the front – *don't* pull your tail thread all the way through, but leave about 20cm (8in) (**Fig.9**). Now come over to the right-hand side and sew from front to back, pass to the left-hand side to the next mark up, and come up from back to front. Continue using your marks in this way to create the lacing until you are at the top left-hand side. Unthread your needle and re-thread it on the long tail thread and bring it through on the top right-hand mark to complete the lacing.

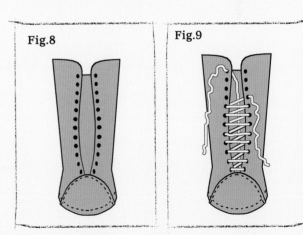

Fig.8   Fig.9

3 Tie the laces in a bow at the top and trim the ends, leaving them long enough to loosen off when you want to change boots. You can remove the boots after you've laced them up, but it's not that easy to get them back on afterwards! It is best to strip out the lacing embroidery and re-do it with a needle.

HOW TO SEW LUNA'S

LACE TOP,
LACE SKIRT AND CROWN

Luna had no idea what she would wear to the Christmas party, but the minute she stepped into the fabric-strewn world of her favourite store the sight of snow-white, scalloped lace fired her imagination. That was it! She would make a dreamy lace set with a full skirt that swished as she danced.

Luna's **grandmother** once said that every **stitch** is a story waiting to happen and **Luna** looked like a **fairytale** heroine as she stepped under the **dazzling** lights of the ball

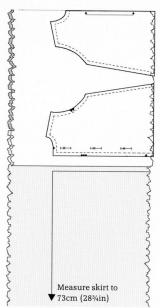

THE LACE TOP
YOU WILL NEED

- Paper pattern for lace top (see The Patterns)
- Deep lace, 120cm (48in) with a depth of at least 15cm (6in) and a scallop on one edge – this amount is sufficient for the top and the skirt
- 100% cotton fabric for lining (for top and skirt), 15cm x 120cm (6in x 48in)
- Three buttons
- Three press studs
- Basic sewing kit (see Materials)

Before you start, refer to The Patterns section for advice on using the patterns.

Measure skirt to
▼ 73cm (28¾in)   **Fig.1**

CUTTING OUT

1 Cut around your paper pattern pieces carefully using scissors. I cut on the black line, but to the outside not the inside. Note that the lace top and skirt pieces are cut from the same piece of fabric – see The Lace Skirt: Cutting Out, step 1 for details on the cutting out for the skirt.

2 Fold over enough of the lace so that you have room to position the top pattern pieces on it – see **Fig.1** as a guide (note that the diagram shows the top and skirt patterns). Pin the pattern pieces onto the lace and cut out. Unpin your pattern pieces and re-cut the pattern in the lining fabric. Mark any notches/triangles with a *tiny* snip in the fabric to the centre of the triangle.

TIP
Take care when ironing lace if it has a high synthetic composition, as it will only take a warm iron.

MAKING UP

Sewing the Shoulders:

1 Take the main fabric pieces and with right sides together, match the shoulder seam of one back to one front shoulder seam. Sew using a 0.5cm (¼in) seam allowance (**Fig.2**). Repeat with the other back piece and the remaining front shoulder seam. Press seams towards the back.

Sewing the Back Edges and Neckline:

1 With right sides together, match the edges of the lining up to the main pieces around the neckline and back edges. Note the lining at the back will finish 1cm (⅜in) shorter than the lace outer because you have made a hem. This should align with a snip you have made in the lace. Pin in place and starting at the lower edge of one back, sew around the edge using a 0.5cm (¼in) seam allowance, finishing at the other lower back. To pivot at a corner, leave the needle down in the fabric, lift the presser foot and swing the fabric to line up with the new angle (**Fig.5**).

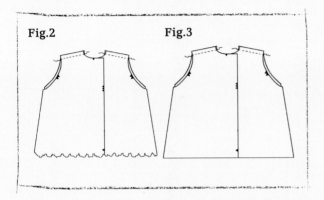

Fig.2   Fig.3

2 Repeat this process with the lining fabric pieces (**Fig.3**).

3 Turn up the hems of the lining pieces towards the right side of the fabric by a scant 0.5cm (¼in) and then another 0.5cm (¼in). Edgestitch in place (**Fig.4**).

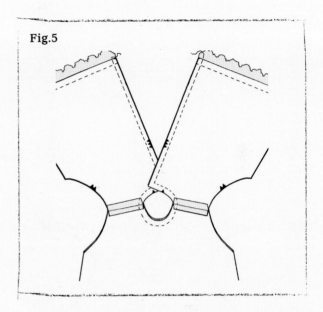

Fig.5

2 Trim excess seam allowances where there are points, and snip into the seam allowance through the neck curve to allow the allowance to sit flat once turned, but don't turn yet (**Fig.6**).

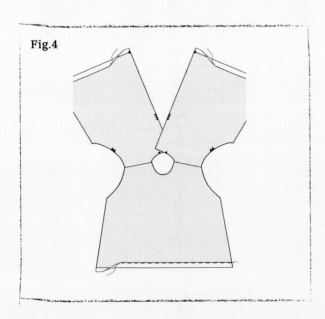

Fig.4

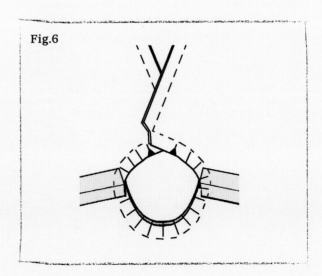

Fig.6

Sewing the Armholes and Side Seams:

1 Pin the lining to the main fabric around each armhole, matching the shoulder seams and edges. Sew each armhole using a 0.5cm (¼in) seam allowance (**Fig.7**). Snip into the allowance on the armholes to allow the allowance to sit flat once turned (**Fig.8**).

3 To sew the side seams work one side at a time. With right (lace) sides together, match the side seams of the outer fabric with the lining, ensuring the armhole seam matches first and then pinning the rest. Sew using a 0.5cm (¼in) seam allowance. Repeat with the other side seam (**Fig.10**). Overlock or zigzag stitch the seam allowance to tidy. Press the side seams to the back. Turn the garment right side out.

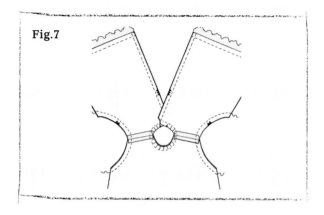

Fig.7

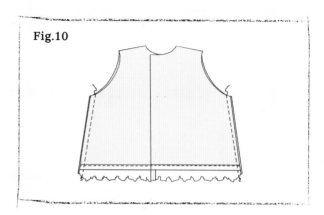

Fig.10

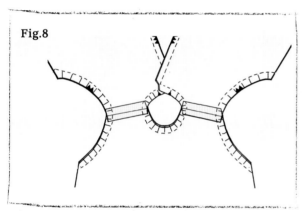

Fig.8

FINISHING OFF

1 Use your original pattern piece to find the button and buttonhole positions. If you are not confident with making buttonholes you can just sew on the buttons and use press studs to fasten. Both methods are given here.

If making buttonholes, mark the button and buttonhole positions on the garment back using the pattern as a guide. Make buttonholes on the left-hand side (as worn). Cut through the buttonholes carefully using an unpicker and a pin at the far end of the buttonhole to ensure you don't rip any further than the buttonhole. Sew the buttons on the right-hand side (as worn) through both the back and back facing.

If using buttons with press studs, sew the buttons on the left-hand side of the garment (as worn) through both the back and back facing. Position one side of a press stud under each button and sew in place. Finish by sewing the other half of each press stud onto the face of the right-hand side (as worn). Well done – Luna's pretty top will be much admired!

2 Push each back through the opening of the shoulder seam to the front and turn through (**Fig.9**). Use a knitting needle to push out the corners. Roll the edges between your fingers and thumb to get the seams on the edge and then press the top back, neck edge and armholes flat.

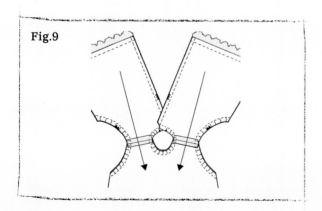

Fig.9

THE LACE SKIRT
YOU WILL NEED

- Paper pattern for lace skirt (see The Patterns)
- Scalloped lace – see Lace Top
- Lining cotton – see Lace Top
- Narrow elastic, 0.5cm (¼in) wide x 22cm (9in)
- Basic sewing kit (see Materials)

Before you start, refer to The Patterns section for advice on using the patterns.

CUTTING OUT

1 The pieces for the skirt are cut at the same time as those for the lace top. Cut the skirt from one piece of lace 73cm (29in) long x 13cm (5in) wide. The lower edge of the lace should still have the scalloped edge on it – do not cut this away. Cut one piece of cotton lining fabric 73cm (29in) long x 13cm (5in) wide.

MAKING UP

1 Make the hem on the cotton lining by turning 0.5cm (¼in) to the right side and then a further 0.5cm (¼in). Press and then edgestitch in place (**Fig.1**).

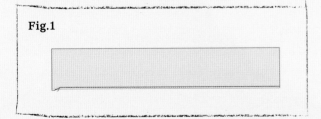

Fig.1

Attaching the Lining to the Outer Skirt:

1 With right sides together match the top of the lace panel to the lining panel and sew together with a 1cm (⅜in) seam (**Fig.2**). Trim the seam allowance to 0.5cm (¼in) and press towards the lace (**Fig.3**).

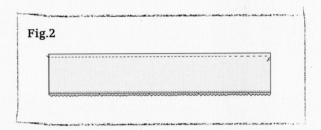

Fig.2

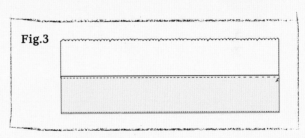

Fig.3

2 Sew the back seam by opening up the panel again and matching the centre back edges. Ensuring the top seam is in line, pin and sew with a 0.5cm (¼in) seam allowance (**Fig.4**). Press the seam open. The panel is now circular.

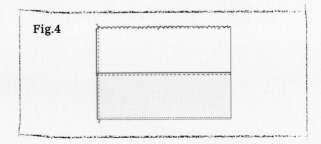

Fig.4

FINISHING OFF

1 To make the casing, create a foldline in the lace about 1.5cm (⅝in) above the seam line where the lining joins the lace. Pin into position all round. Topstitch 1cm (⅜in) down from the folded edge, starting at centre back and finishing 2.5cm (1in) away, to leave an opening for the elastic (**Fig.5**). Edgestitch around the top edge, about 2mm (¹⁄₁₆in) from the folded edge.

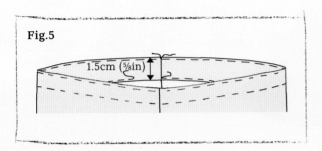

Fig.5

1.5cm (⅝in)

2 Put a safety pin through one end of the elastic and close the pin. Find the opening between the lace and the lining and thread the elastic through the casing, ensuring that the unthreaded end of the elastic is still accessible. Adjust the gathering around the waist to be even. Overlap the two elastic ends by 2cm (¾in) and join using a zigzag machine stitch. Pull the waistband out so the elastic disappears into the casing. Finish by closing the casing opening with machine stitching.

THE LACE CROWN
YOU WILL NEED

- Scrap of skinny lace
- PVA glue
- Plastic container for glue
- Spoon
- Embellishments of your choice, such as tiny flowers, beads or glitter
- Basic sewing kit (see Materials)

MAKING UP

1 The lace piece needs to be about 2cm x 20cm (¾in x 8in). Start by stiffening the lace, as follows. In a small cup, mix about a dessertspoon of PVA glue with a teaspoon of water to thin it down. Push the lace into it and stir with the spoon to coat the lace.

2 Take the lace out and squeeze it to remove excess glue. Lay it onto something flat and plastic, for example, an ice-cream tub lid. Straighten the lace out so it retains its open weave and has a straight edge. Wash your hands (unless you love that peeling-glue-off-your-fingers business!). Allow to dry in a warm place for an hour – separating the lace from the plastic before it dries out completely.

3 Trim the lace to 18cm (7in) long. Overlap one end over the other by 1cm (⅜in) to form a ring and sew together using small hand stitches.

4 If you wish, add some tiny flowers, or some glitter, and when dry, pop over Luna's ears for a festival look.

HOW TO SEW LUNA'S

WINTER CAPE

Inside Luna's favourite haberdashery store was every imaginable colour – surely here she would find that extra something for her party outfit. And then inspiration struck as she spied a flash of woollen red, the deep cherry red of Christmas. She would make a glorious red cape with a tiny bobtail trim all around the edge.

Everywhere she looked there
was fabric in *quirky* prints and
every possible **polka** dot, buttons
that looked like *flowers* and ribbons
so **pretty** they made her heart *sing*

YOU WILL NEED

- Paper pattern for cape (see The Patterns)
- Outer fabric, 32cm x 72cm (13in x 28in) – I chose red but you could use any colour
- Brushed cotton lining, 32cm x 72cm (13in x 28in)
- Pompom trim, 1.5m (1¾yd)
- Hook and eye
- Machine zipper foot
- Basic sewing kit (see Materials)

Before you start, refer to The Patterns section for advice on using the patterns.

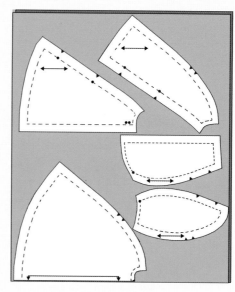

Fig.1

CUTTING OUT

1 Cut around your paper pattern pieces carefully. I cut on the black line, but to the outside not the inside. Seam allowances are included.

2 Pin the pattern pieces onto the fabric, using **Fig.1** as a guide and noting which pieces should be cut in which fabric. Cut out the pieces and transfer any markings. Mark any notches/triangles with a *tiny* snip to the centre of the triangle. Unpin your pattern pieces from the outer fabric and repeat the process with the lining. These fabrics have a right and a wrong side (shown in the illustrations and referred to in the instructions). Because the item is fully lined you don't need to finish raw edges.

MAKING UP

Making the Hood:

1 Sew the hood side seams on the outer and lining as follows. With right sides together, match one outer front hood with one outer back hood, matching the notches. Pin and sew with a 1cm (⅜in) seam allowance from the top to the level of the first notch (**Fig.2**). Now resume your sewing from the second notch to the bottom.

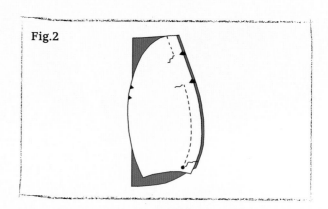

Fig.2

2 Repeat this with the other hood pieces, remembering to make them symmetrical (**Fig.3**). Press the seam allowance open and flat, including where you have left an opening (**Fig.4**).

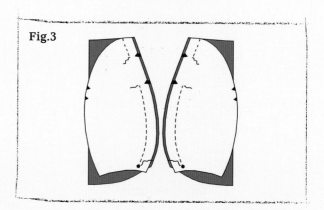

Fig.3

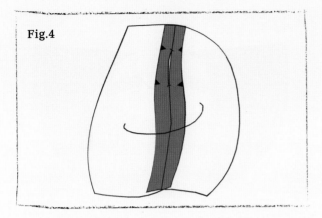

Fig.4

3 Repeat these steps with the corresponding lining pieces. Tack (baste) around each opening to hold the seam allowances back for when you finish these later (**Fig.5**).

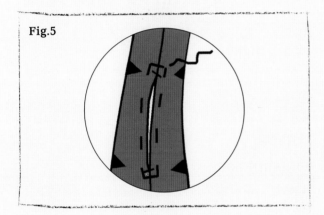

Fig.5

4 Sew the hood overhead seam for the outer and lining as follows. With right sides together, take the two outer hood pieces and match them up, taking care that the side seams match along the top. Pin and then sew using a 1cm (⅜in) seam allowance (**Fig.6**). Repeat with the two lining hood pieces. Press the seams open and flat and then set aside.

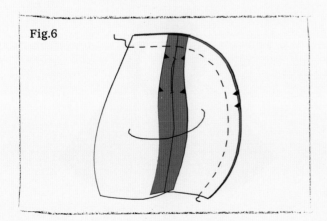

Fig.6

Making the Cape:
1 Sew the front to the side fronts for the outer and lining as follows. With right sides together, match one front outer to one side front outer, matching the notches. Pin and sew with a 1cm (⅜in) seam allowance from the top to the level of the first notch. Now resume your sewing from the second notch to the bottom (**Fig.7**). Repeat with the other outer front and side front pieces, remembering to make them symmetrical. Press the seam allowance open and flat, including where you have left an opening (**Fig.8**).

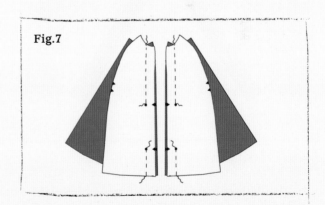

Fig.7

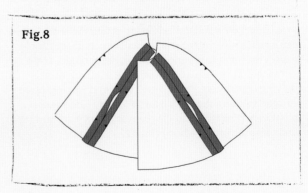

Fig.8

WINTER CAPE

2 Repeat these steps with the corresponding lining pieces. Tack (baste) around each opening to hold the seam allowances back until you finish these later.

3 Sew the shoulder seams on the outer and lining as follows. With right sides together, lay the back panel upwards and then match a front panel to each side. Sew each side using a 1cm (⅜in) seam allowance (**Fig.9**). Repeat with the lining front and back *but* on one side only, leaving an opening of 7cm (2¾in) as in **Fig.10** – this is for turning everything through later. Press seams open.

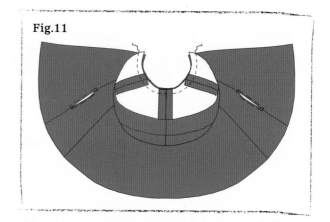

Fig.11

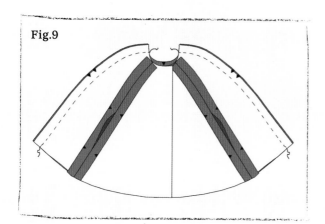

Fig.9

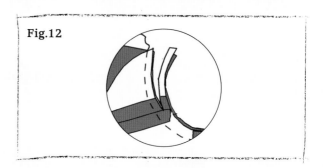

Fig.12

5 Repeat this process with the lining hood and the lining main body.

FINISHING OFF

1 Working with the outer cape, pin and then tack (baste) the pompom trim all around the outer edge of the hood, the front edges and the hem. The pompom should be facing inwards and the tape part should be just inside the raw edge of the cape (**Fig.13**). Where you have to turn a corner, snip the tape of the pompom to allow it to turn the corner. Where your pompom edges meet, you can just run the ends off to overlap and come behind the 1cm (⅜in) stitching line.

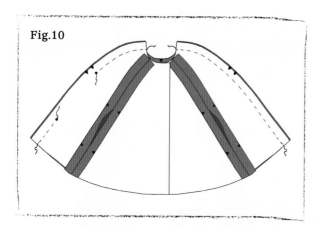

Fig.10

4 Attach the hood to the main body on the outer and the lining as follows. With right sides together, pin the hood neck edge to the main body of the cape. You will be able to use the back seam of the hood to match the notch at the centre back and the front edges will match up too. Don't expect the hood side panel to match the shoulder seam as this has been displaced to stop the seam allowance making it too bulky. Pin and tack (baste) if you feel more comfortable and then sew using a 0.5cm (¼in) seam allowance (**Fig.11**). Trim the seam allowance to 3mm (⅛in) and press towards the hood (**Fig.12**).

Fig.13

2 To finish the outer edges, with right sides together, match up the lining to the outer, enclosing the pompom trim. Pin and then sew with a 1cm (⅜in) seam allowance (**Fig.14**) using a zipper foot on the machine (with the needle to the left-hand side of the foot). The zipper foot will allow you to get close to the bulk of the pompom trim. Take your time and really focus on the seam allowance being correct as you sew all the way around the cape.

4 Match the outer openings you have made for the ears and the arms to the openings in the linings and slipstitch the outer to the lining around each one. Remove the tacking (basting) threads. Slipstitch the opening in the lining shoulder seam together. Using a double thread, attach the hook and eye to the front edges, as marked on the pattern, but on the lining side, so the cape will stay edge to edge when the hook and eye are fastened. Luna's gorgeous cape is now ready to wear.

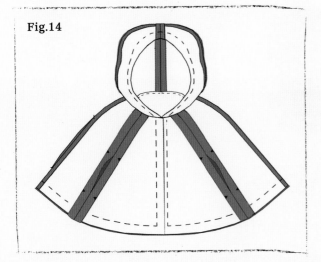

Fig.14

3 Trim the seam allowance from the front corners to reduce the bulk when you turn through. Turn through using the opening in the lining, poke any corners out well and then press flat (**Fig.15**). It is **very** important to turn your iron temperature down, otherwise the pompoms may melt!

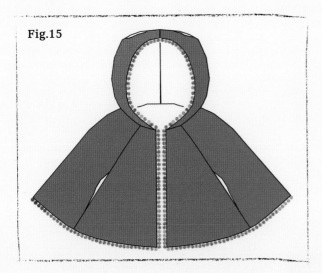

Fig.15

HOW TO SEW LUNA'S

PYJAMAS

That night, with sore paws from too much dancing, Luna flopped on to her little bed. She let out a sigh of contentment and hopefulness for the New Year to come, and then slipped out of her party clothes into her strawberry printed PJs and was soon drifting off to sleep.

Cosy PJs and a warm *bed* were all that were

needed for a **peaceful** night *dreaming*

of eating **wildflower** salad with

her brothers and **sisters** in their

warm **burrow** at home

YOU WILL NEED

- Paper pattern for pyjamas (see The Patterns)
- Fat quarter of printed 100% cotton
- 1.5m (1½yd) pre-folded lace-edged bias binding (see Suppliers)
- Elastic, 0.5cm (¼in) wide x 22cm (9in)
- Safety pin
- Two press studs
- Basic sewing kit (see Materials)

Before you start, refer to The Patterns section for advice on using the patterns.

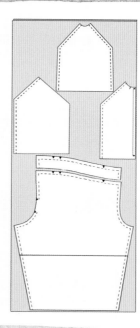

Fig.1

CUTTING OUT

1 Cut around your paper pattern pieces carefully using scissors. I cut on the black line, but to the outside not the inside.

2 Join the upper and lower leg pieces together using adhesive tape. Fold the fabric in half so that right sides are together. Pin your pattern pieces onto the fabric, using **Fig.1** as a guide and cut out the pieces carefully. Mark any notches/triangles with a *tiny* snip in the fabric to the centre of the triangle.

TIP
If you don't have any lace-edged bias binding you can use this technique on normal bias. Press it in half along the length with a warm iron and then use as in these instructions.

MAKING UP

Making the Pyjama Top:

1 Enclose the hem of each sleeve piece with the bias binding. You will be able to just open up the fold, pop in the raw edge of the fabric and then close the bias over it. Sew through all layers with an edgestitch, about 2mm (¹⁄₁₆in) from the folded edge of the bias (**Fig.2**). Trim excess bias from the edges to be in line with the sleeve shape.

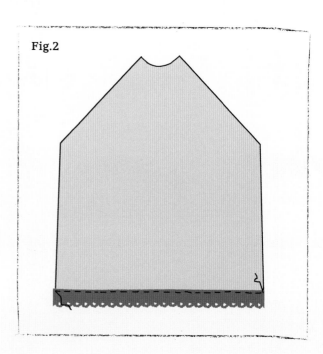

Fig.2

2 With right sides together, match one back sleeve seam to one sleeve seam. Sew together with a 0.5cm (¼in) seam allowance (**Fig.3**). Repeat with the other back sleeve seam and other sleeve (**Fig.4**).

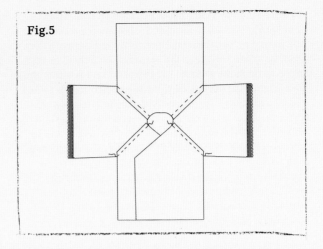

Fig.5

4 With right sides together, match up the sleeve seams, underarm and side seams and pin in place. Sew 0.5cm (¼in) away from the edge as in **Fig.6**. Press the seams towards the back of the top as far as you can. Snip the fabric once at the underarm and turn the top inside out.

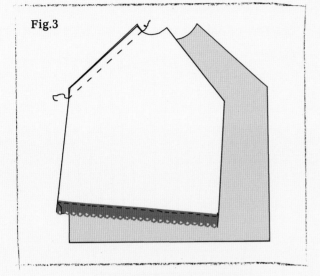

Fig.3

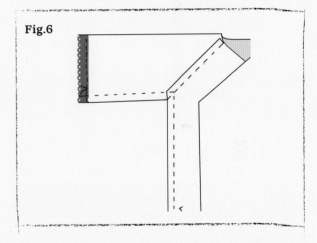

Fig.6

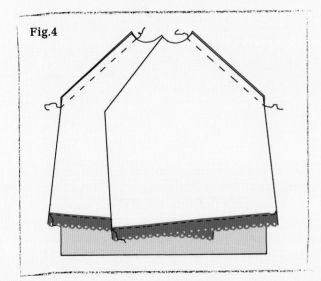

Fig.4

5 Enclose the hem of the top with the bias binding. Open up the fold, pop in the raw edge of the fabric and then close the bias over it. Sew through all layers with an edgestitch about 2mm (¹⁄₁₆in) from the folded edge of the bias (**Fig.7**).

3 Join the front sleeve seams to the remaining free sleeve seams in the same way (**Fig.5**). Press all sleeve seams towards the sleeve.

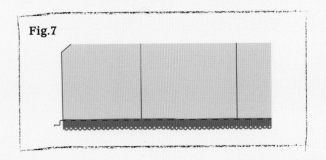

Fig.7

6 Turn a small amount of the bias to the inside, about 1cm (⅜in). Position the bias at the bottom front corner of one front. Enclose the straight edge of the front with the binding. When you reach the corner, stretch the bias on its lacy edge to make a curve. Pin as you go, and position the bias around the neck edge, this time stretching the folded plain edge of the bias to cope with the neck edge curve. Come back down the other front, repeating the method of going around the corner on the front. When you can see how much bias you will need to complete the remaining front edge, cut it about 1cm (⅜in) longer, turn the end to the inside and pin the bias in place on the front edge. You could baste (tack) the bias in place before sewing. Sew through all layers with an edgestitch about 2mm (¹⁄₁₆in) from the folded edge of the bias (**Fig.8**).

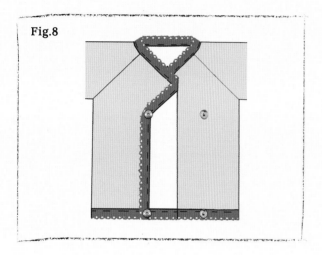

Fig.8

7 Using your pattern piece, mark the positions for sewing on the press studs. Pyjamas for a girl rabbit will wrap with the right-hand side on the top (as worn), and the opposite way for a boy rabbit. Sew the top press studs without letting your stitching be visible on the right side of the garment (**Fig.9**).

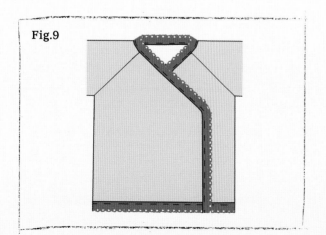

Fig.9

Making the Pyjama Bottoms:

1 Enclose the hem of each leg piece with the bias binding, as before. Sew through all layers with an edgestitch, about 2mm (¹⁄₁₆in) from the folded edge of the bias (**Fig.10**). Now trim extra bias from the edges to be in line with the leg shape.

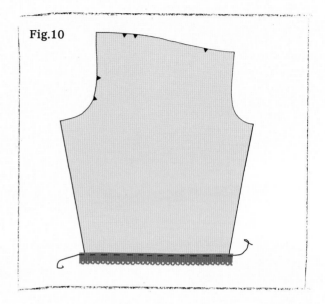

Fig.10

2 Working one leg at a time, with right sides together, match the inside leg seams and sew with a 0.5cm (¼in) seam allowance (**Fig.11**). Repeat with the other leg. Press the seams towards the back of the leg.

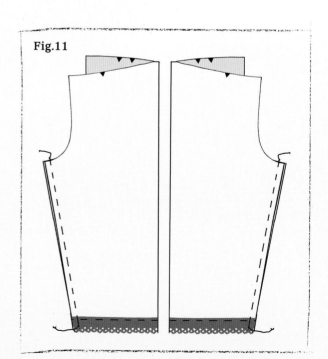

Fig.11

3 Turn one leg to be right side out and slide it, lower edge first, inside the other leg to sew the crotch. Matching edges and notches and inside leg seam, pin and sew the crotch with a 0.5cm (¼in) seam allowance, leaving an opening in the seam between the notches for the tail (**Fig.12**).

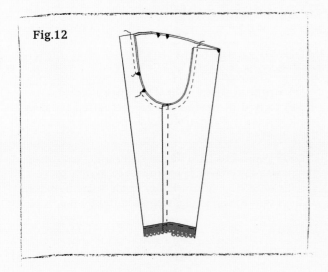

Fig.12

4 For the facing, with right sides together, join the short edges of the front facing with a 0.5cm (¼in) seam allowance and press open (**Fig.13**). With right sides together, join the short edges of the back facing with a 0.5cm (¼in) seam allowance and press open. Your facing will now be a circular loop. Press the lower edge of the facing (no notches) up to the wrong side by 0.5cm (¼in) all round (**Fig.14**).

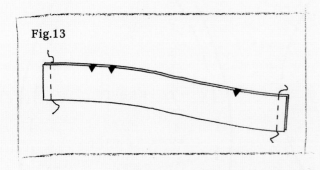

Fig.13

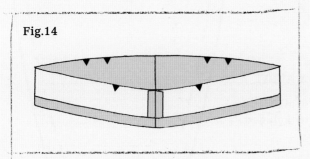

Fig.14

5 With right sides together, match up the edges of the waist to the facing using the notches and seams and sew together using a 0.5cm (¼in) seam allowance (**Fig.15**).

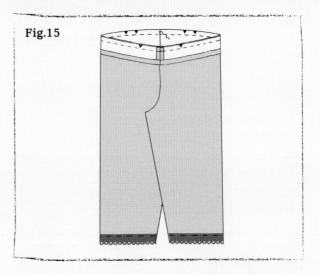

Fig.15

6 For the casing, turn the facing to the inside, press and pin in place. Edgestitch around the top edge. Topstitch 1cm (⅜in) down from the top edge, starting at the centre back and finishing about 2.5cm (1in) away to leave an opening for threading the elastic (**Fig.16**).

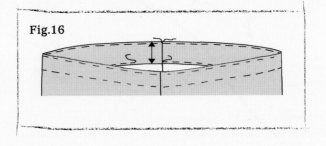

Fig.16

FINISHING OFF

1 Put a safety pin through one end of the elastic and close the pin. Thread the elastic through the casing, ensuring that the unthreaded end of the elastic is still accessible.

2 Adjust the gathering around the waist to be even and then trim 2.5cm (1in) from the end of the elastic. Overlap the two elastic ends by 2.5cm (1in) and join using a zigzag machine stitch. Pull the waistband so the elastic disappears into the casing. Close the casing opening with machine stitching. Time for a cozy night's sleep!

THE PATTERNS

The patterns for the projects have been supplied full size.

When using patterns follow these general guidelines.

Refer to the pattern layout diagram with each project to see which patterns are needed.

All patterns should be photocopied at 100%.

The patterns have seam allowances included (not always to scale). The allowances are stated in the project instructions.

Before cutting, iron the patterns and your fabric to remove any creases.

Once copied, cut your paper patterns out first before you pin them onto the fabric. Cut around your paper pattern pieces carefully. I cut on the black line, but to the *outside* of the line, not the inside.

Some patterns are only half of the shape and these are clearly marked. In these cases, place the marked line along the fold of the fabric, so when the shape is cut out you will have doubled the pattern.

Cutting out is crucial to success so the use of pins when positioning a pattern on fabric will really improve your results. When pinning keep the entire pin *inside* the pattern so there is no danger of your scissors hitting the pin.

You will see symbols on the patterns – some of the common ones are shown and explained here.

⟵——⟶ Fabric grain

– – – – Sewing line

▼ ❙ ● Triangle/notch and dot position markers

╳ Buttonhole and button positions

Place on fold of fabric

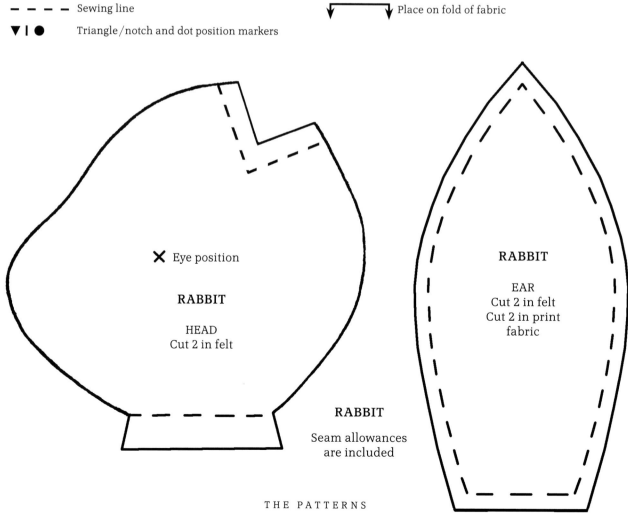

✕ Eye position

RABBIT

HEAD
Cut 2 in felt

RABBIT

Seam allowances
are included

RABBIT

EAR
Cut 2 in felt
Cut 2 in print
fabric

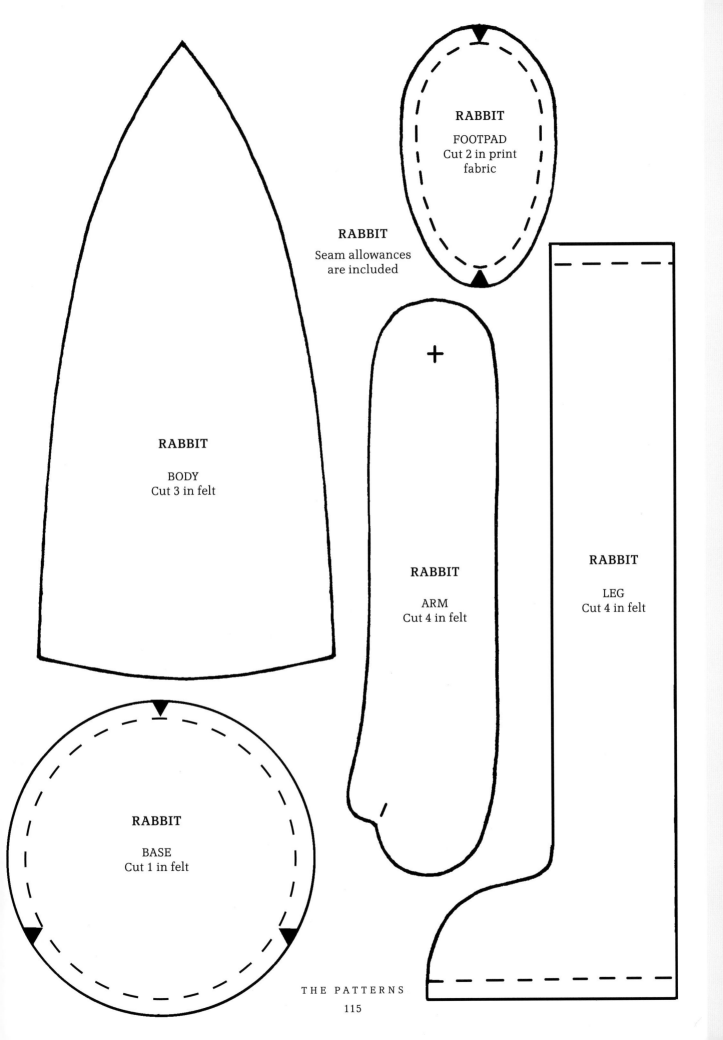

RABBIT

FOOTPAD
Cut 2 in print
fabric

RABBIT

Seam allowances
are included

RABBIT

BODY
Cut 3 in felt

RABBIT

ARM
Cut 4 in felt

RABBIT

LEG
Cut 4 in felt

RABBIT

BASE
Cut 1 in felt

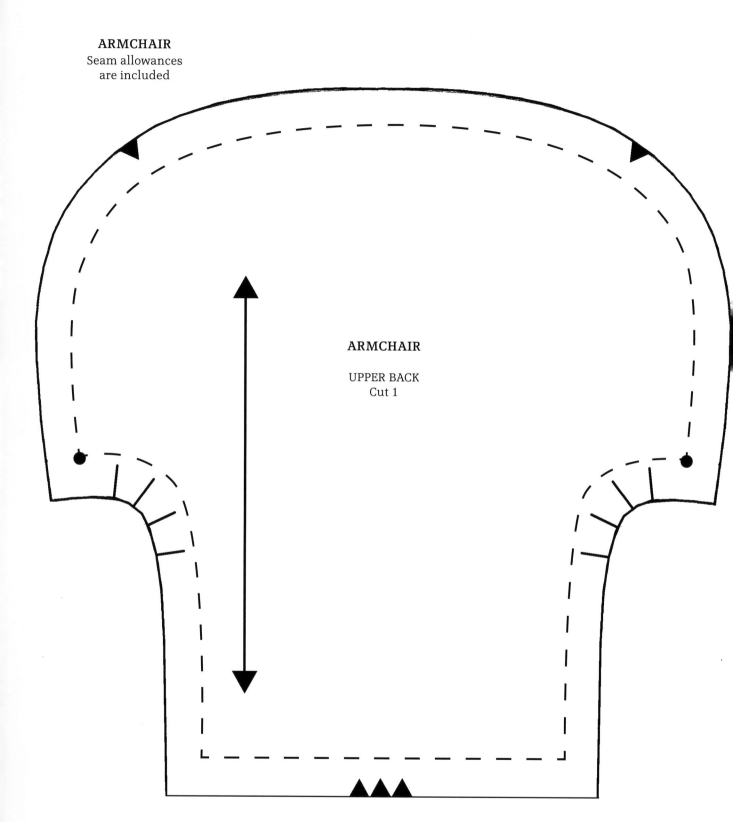

ARMCHAIR
Seam allowances
are included

ARMCHAIR

UPPER BACK
Cut 1

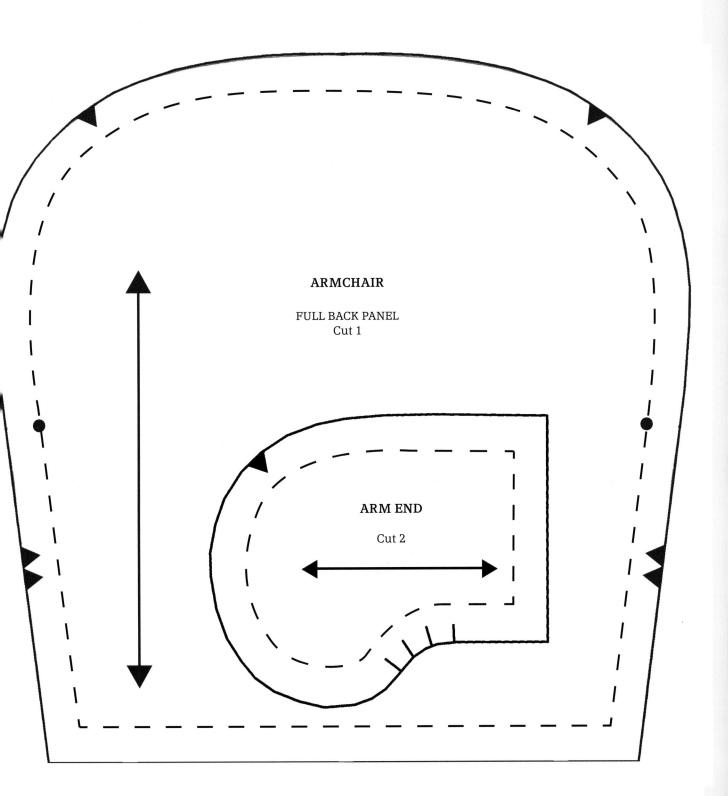

ARMCHAIR

FULL BACK PANEL
Cut 1

ARM END

Cut 2

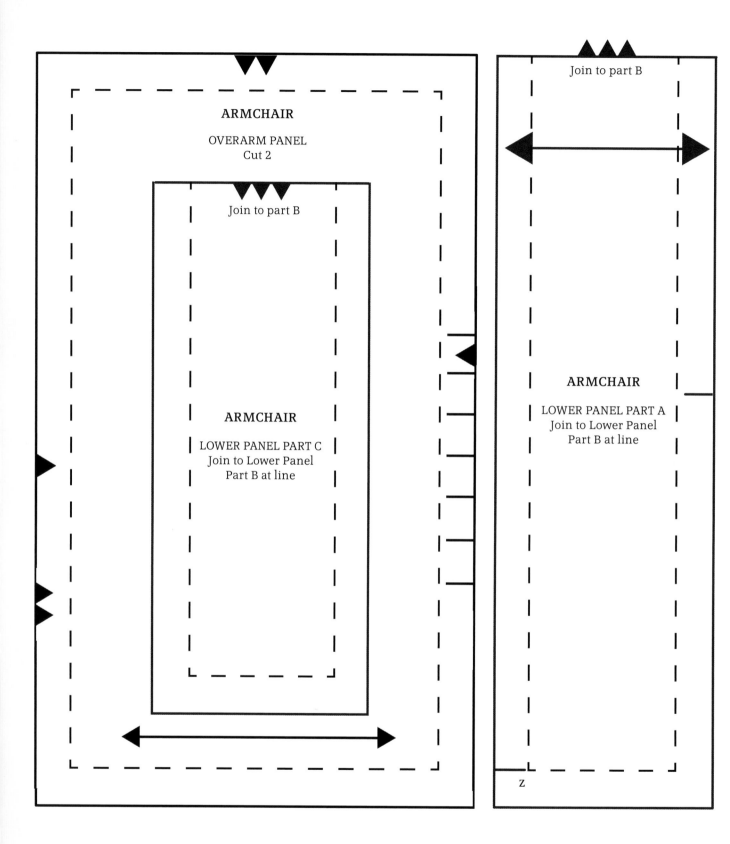

ARMCHAIR

OVERARM PANEL
Cut 2

Join to part B

ARMCHAIR

LOWER PANEL PART C
Join to Lower Panel
Part B at line

Join to part B

ARMCHAIR

LOWER PANEL PART A
Join to Lower Panel
Part B at line

Z

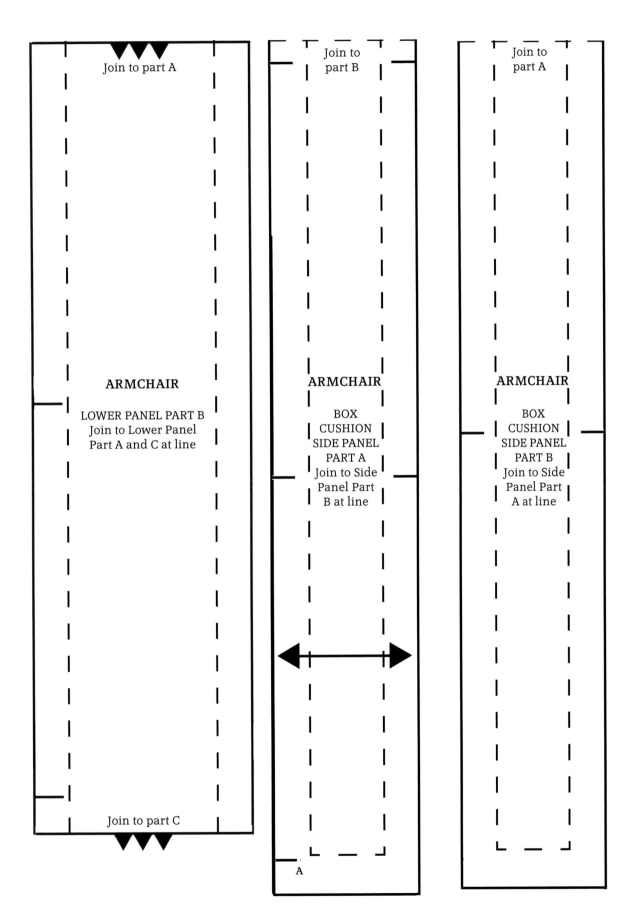

Join to part A

ARMCHAIR

LOWER PANEL PART B
Join to Lower Panel
Part A and C at line

Join to part C

Join to
part B

ARMCHAIR

BOX
CUSHION
SIDE PANEL
PART A
Join to Side
Panel Part
B at line

A

Join to
part A

ARMCHAIR

BOX
CUSHION
SIDE PANEL
PART B
Join to Side
Panel Part
A at line

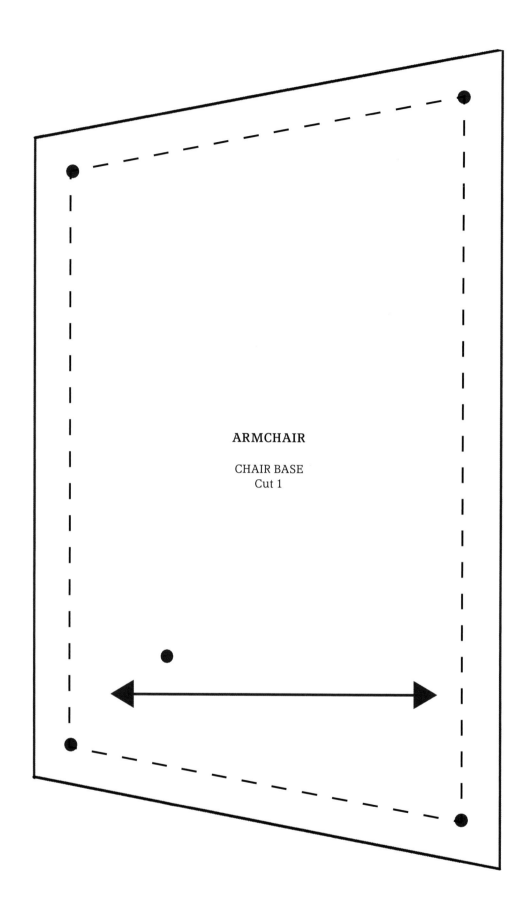

ARMCHAIR

CHAIR BASE
Cut 1

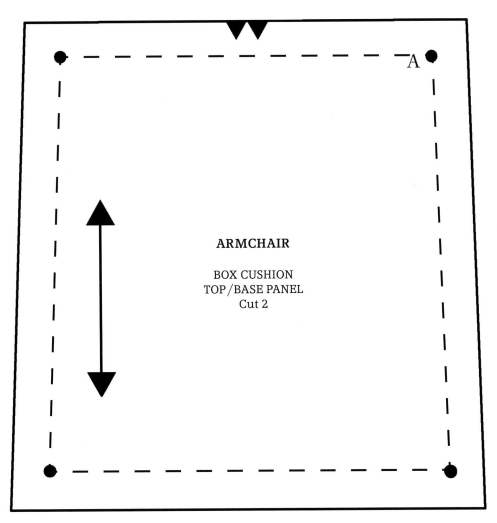

ARMCHAIR

BOX CUSHION
TOP/BASE PANEL
Cut 2

A

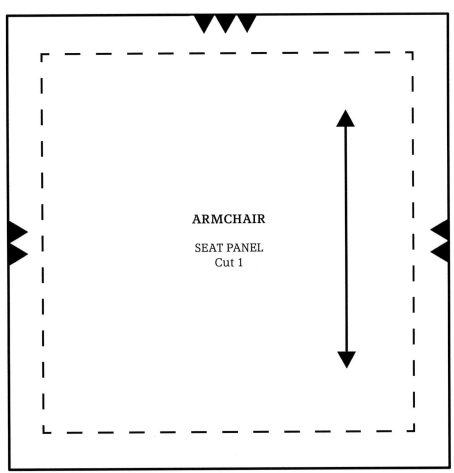

ARMCHAIR

SEAT PANEL
Cut 1

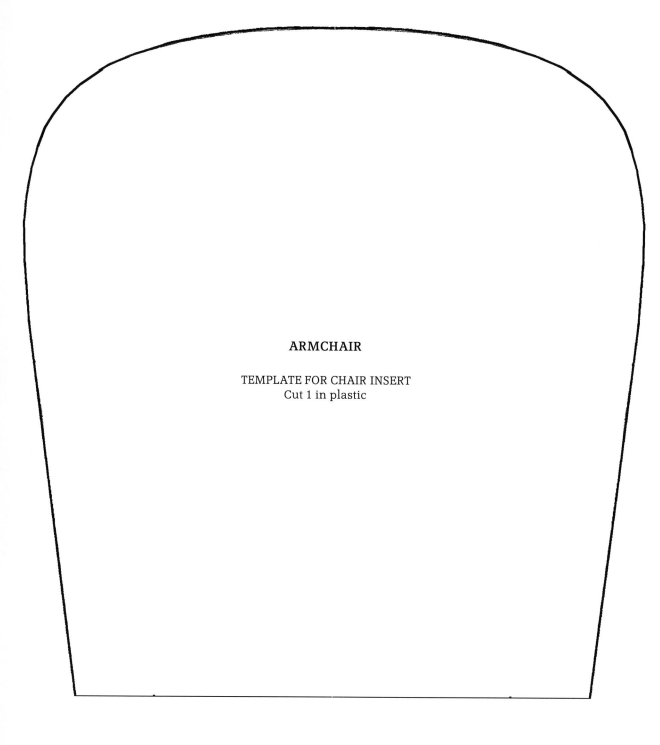

ARMCHAIR

TEMPLATE FOR CHAIR INSERT
Cut 1 in plastic

T-SHIRT DRESS
Seam allowances
are included

Snip

Snip

T-SHIRT DRESS

COLLAR
Cut 1

Snip

Snip

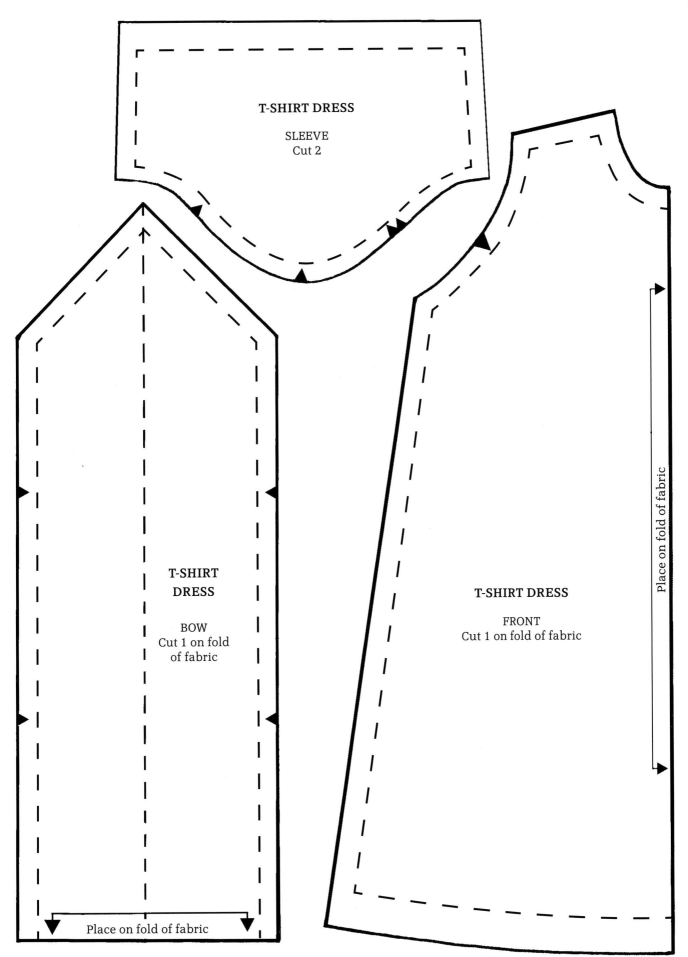

T-SHIRT DRESS

SLEEVE
Cut 2

T-SHIRT DRESS

BOW
Cut 1 on fold
of fabric

T-SHIRT DRESS

FRONT
Cut 1 on fold of fabric

Place on fold of fabric

Place on fold of fabric

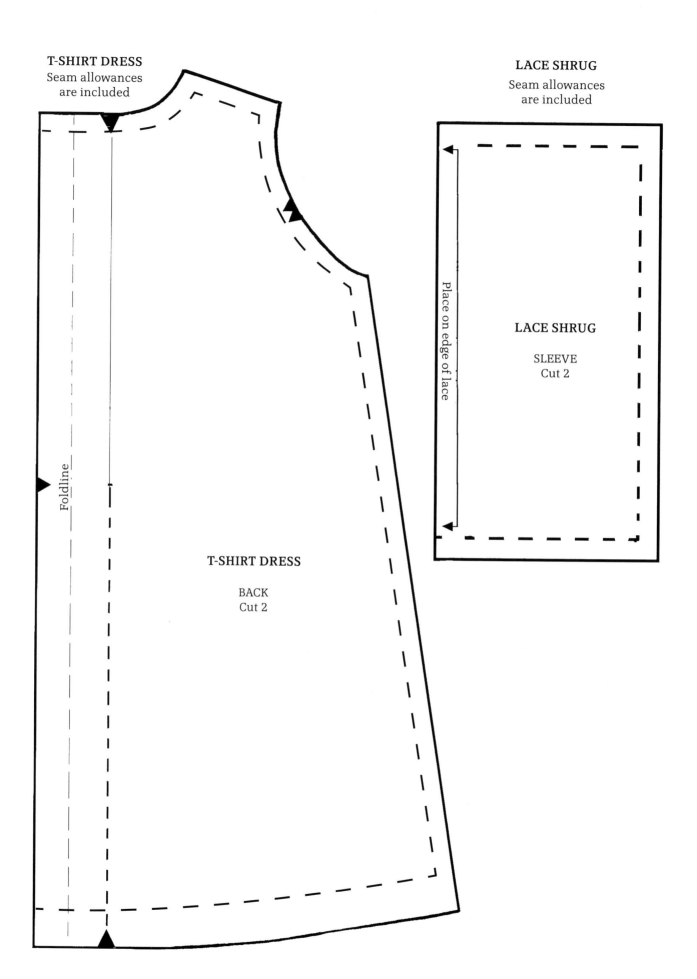

T-SHIRT DRESS
Seam allowances
are included

Foldline

T-SHIRT DRESS

BACK
Cut 2

LACE SHRUG
Seam allowances
are included

Place on edge of lace

LACE SHRUG

SLEEVE
Cut 2

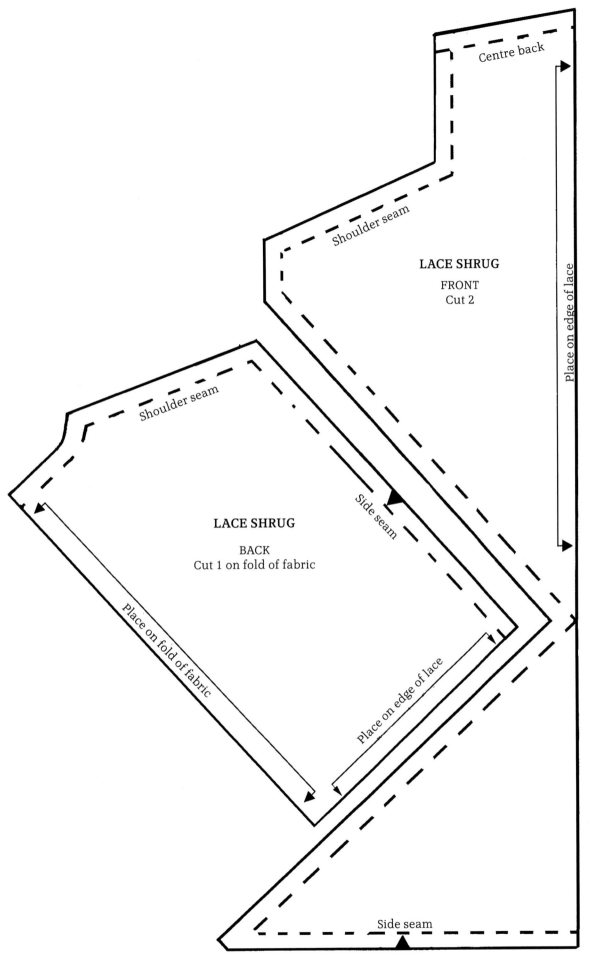

LACE SHRUG

FRONT
Cut 2

Centre back

Place on edge of lace

Shoulder seam

Shoulder seam

Side seam

LACE SHRUG

BACK
Cut 1 on fold of fabric

Place on fold of fabric

Place on edge of lace

Side seam

THE PATTERNS

125

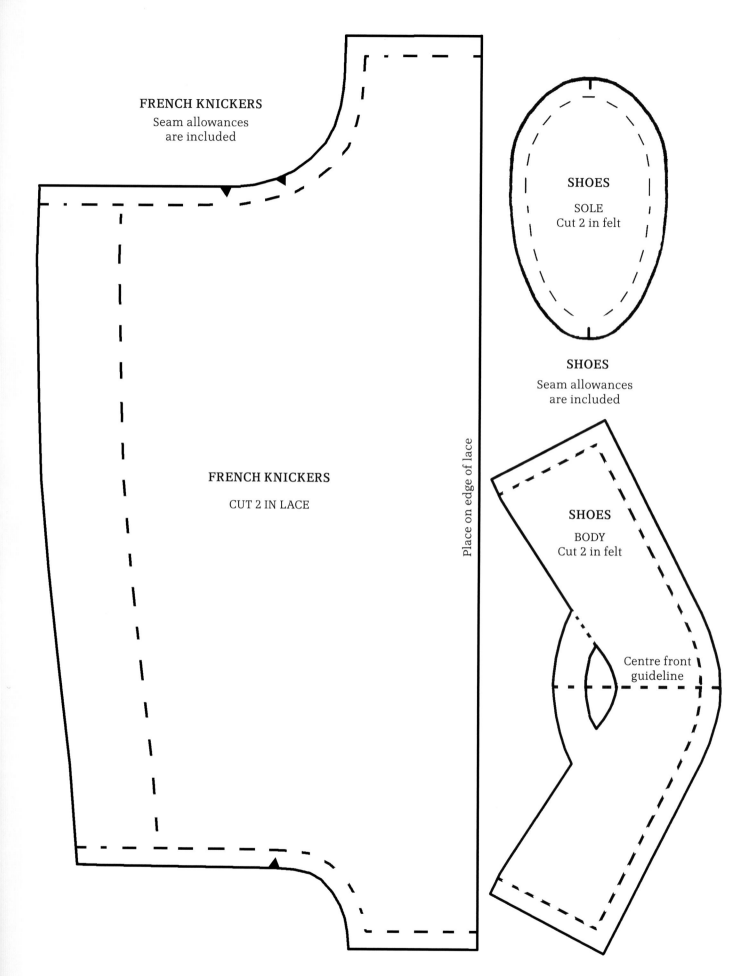

FRENCH KNICKERS

Seam allowances
are included

FRENCH KNICKERS

CUT 2 IN LACE

Place on edge of lace

SHOES

SOLE
Cut 2 in felt

SHOES

Seam allowances
are included

SHOES

BODY
Cut 2 in felt

Centre front
guideline

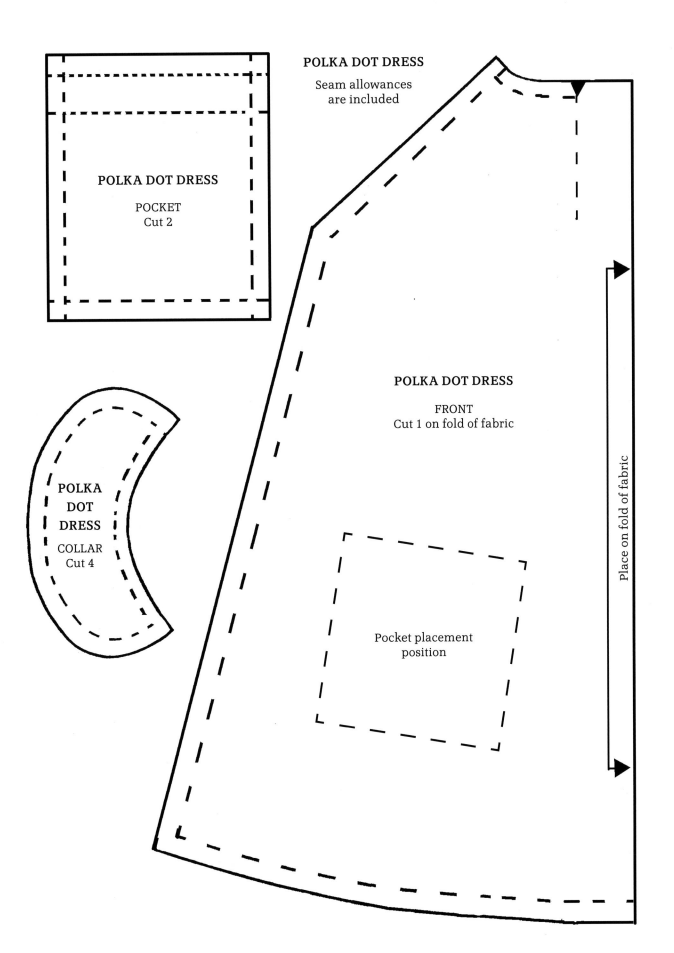

POLKA DOT DRESS

Seam allowances are included

POLKA DOT DRESS

POCKET
Cut 2

POLKA
DOT
DRESS

COLLAR
Cut 4

POLKA DOT DRESS

FRONT
Cut 1 on fold of fabric

Place on fold of fabric

Pocket placement
position

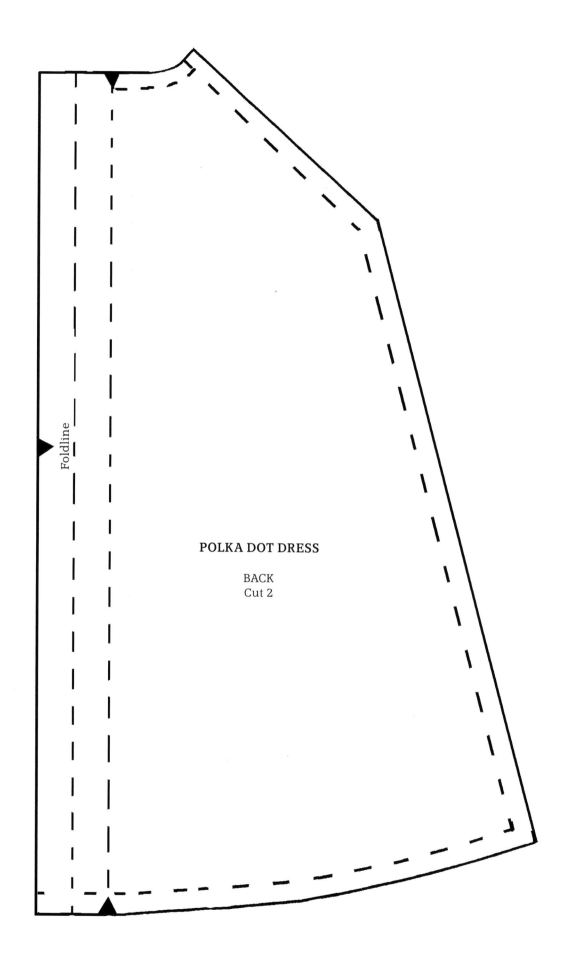

Foldline

POLKA DOT DRESS

BACK
Cut 2

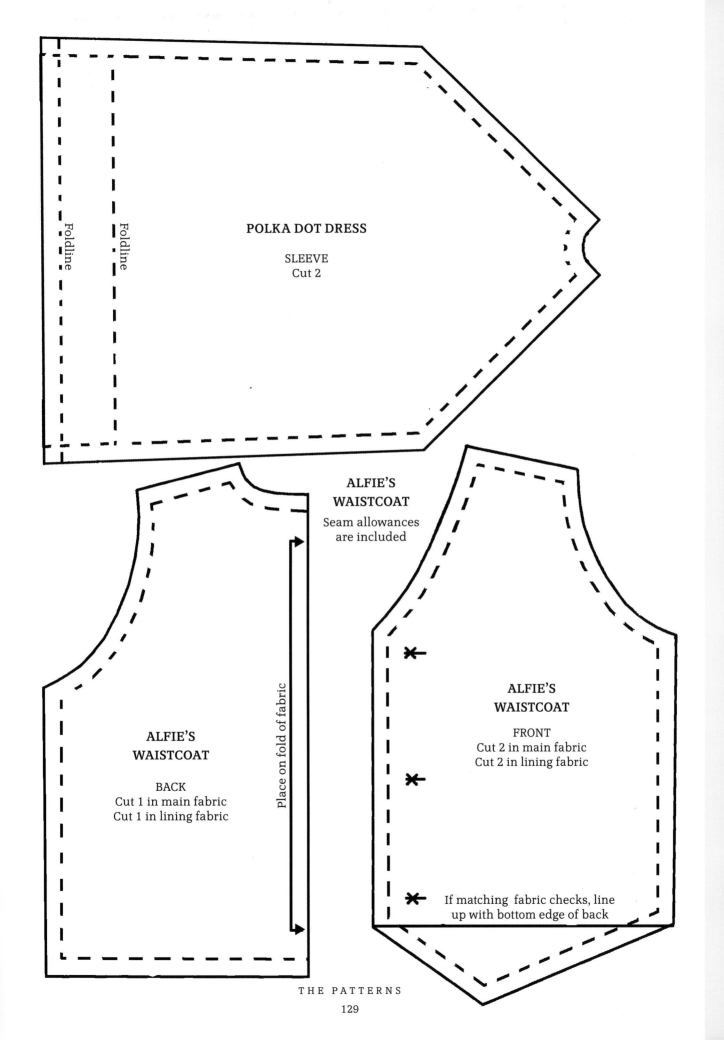

POLKA DOT DRESS

SLEEVE
Cut 2

Foldline

Foldline

**ALFIE'S
WAISTCOAT**

Seam allowances
are included

Place on fold of fabric

**ALFIE'S
WAISTCOAT**

BACK
Cut 1 in main fabric
Cut 1 in lining fabric

**ALFIE'S
WAISTCOAT**

FRONT
Cut 2 in main fabric
Cut 2 in lining fabric

If matching fabric checks, line
up with bottom edge of back

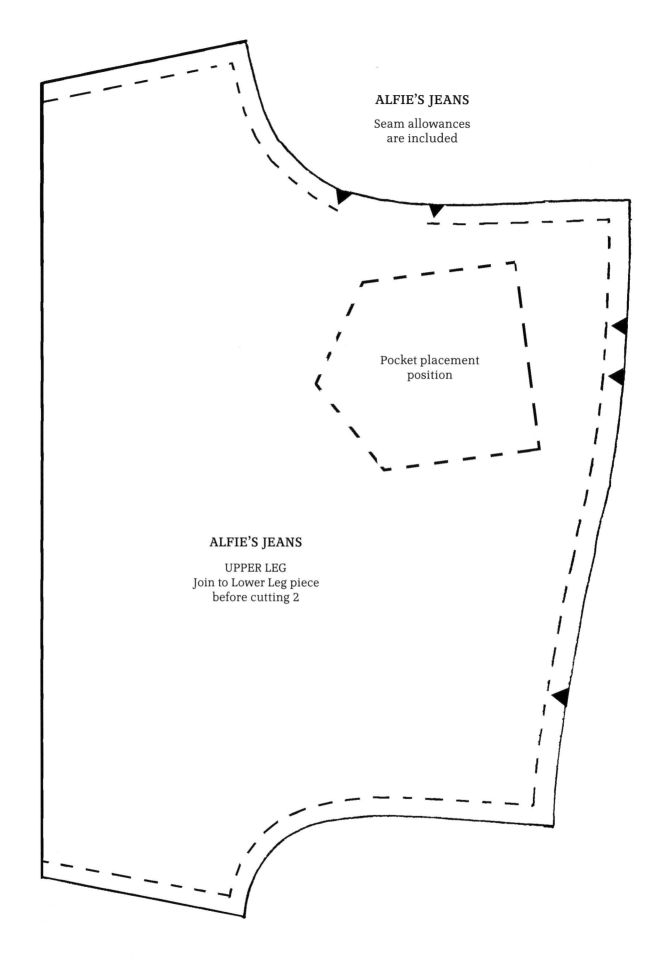

ALFIE'S JEANS

Seam allowances
are included

Pocket placement
position

ALFIE'S JEANS

UPPER LEG
Join to Lower Leg piece
before cutting 2

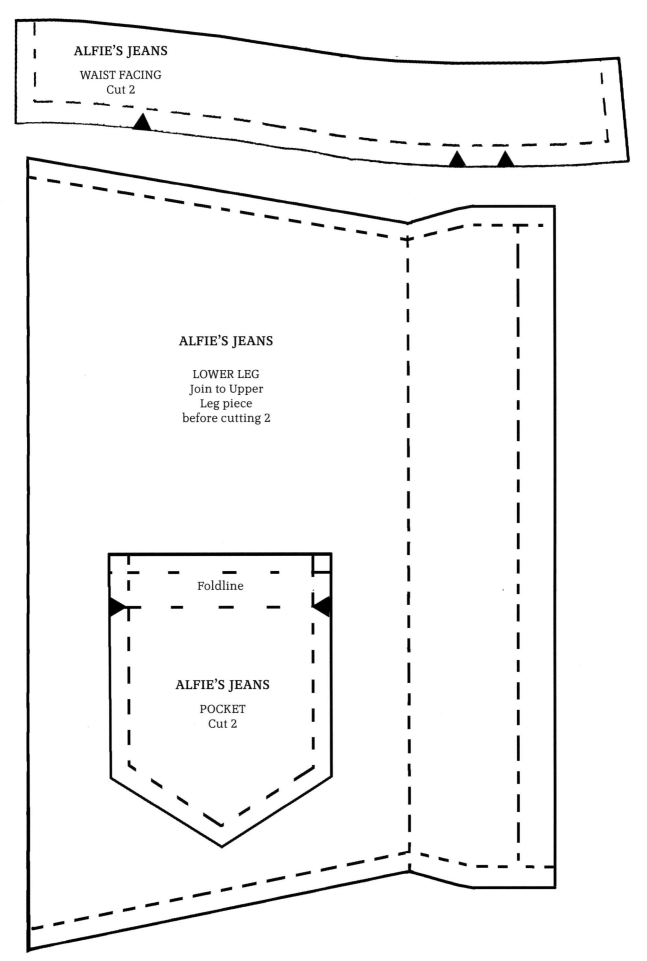

ALFIE'S JEANS

WAIST FACING
Cut 2

ALFIE'S JEANS

LOWER LEG
Join to Upper
Leg piece
before cutting 2

Foldline

ALFIE'S JEANS

POCKET
Cut 2

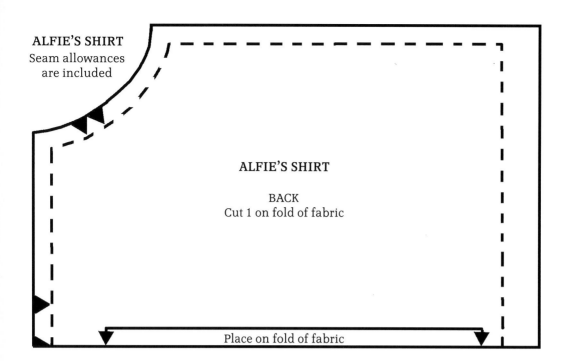

ALFIE'S SHIRT
Seam allowances
are included

ALFIE'S SHIRT

BACK
Cut 1 on fold of fabric

Place on fold of fabric

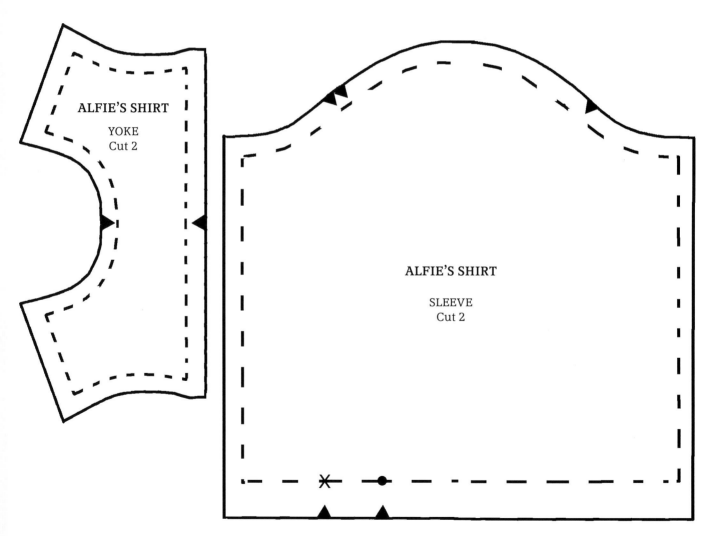

ALFIE'S SHIRT

YOKE
Cut 2

ALFIE'S SHIRT

SLEEVE
Cut 2

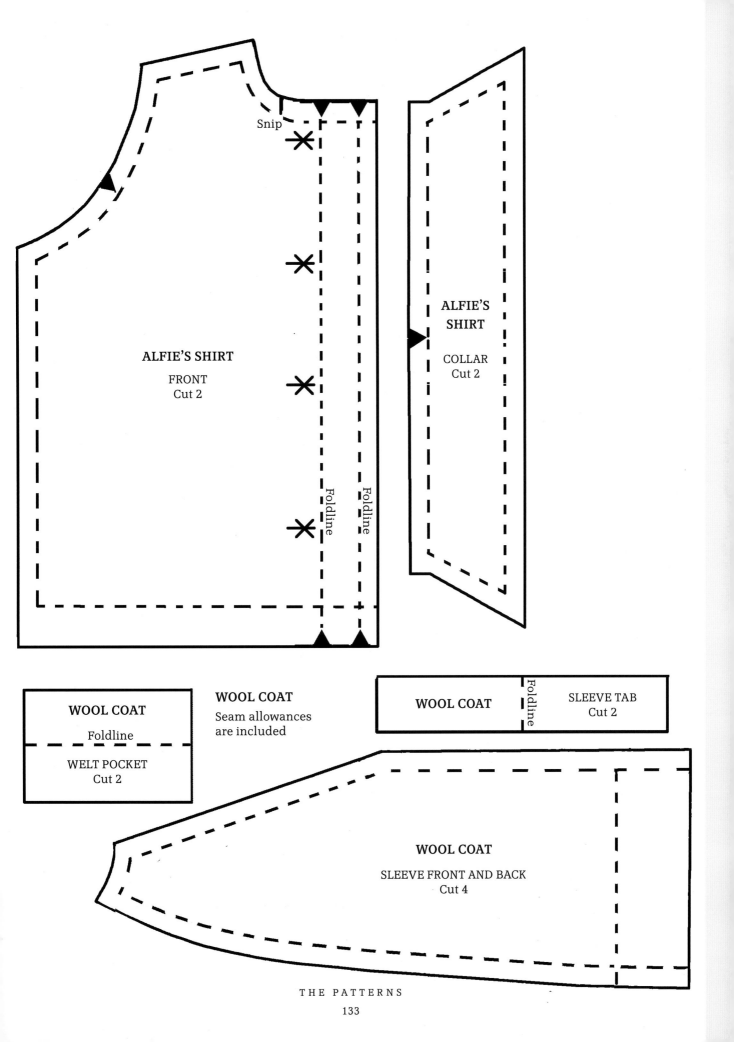

Snip

ALFIE'S SHIRT

FRONT
Cut 2

Foldline

Foldline

ALFIE'S
SHIRT

COLLAR
Cut 2

WOOL COAT

Foldline

WELT POCKET
Cut 2

WOOL COAT

Seam allowances
are included

WOOL COAT

Foldline

SLEEVE TAB
Cut 2

WOOL COAT

SLEEVE FRONT AND BACK
Cut 4

THE PATTERNS

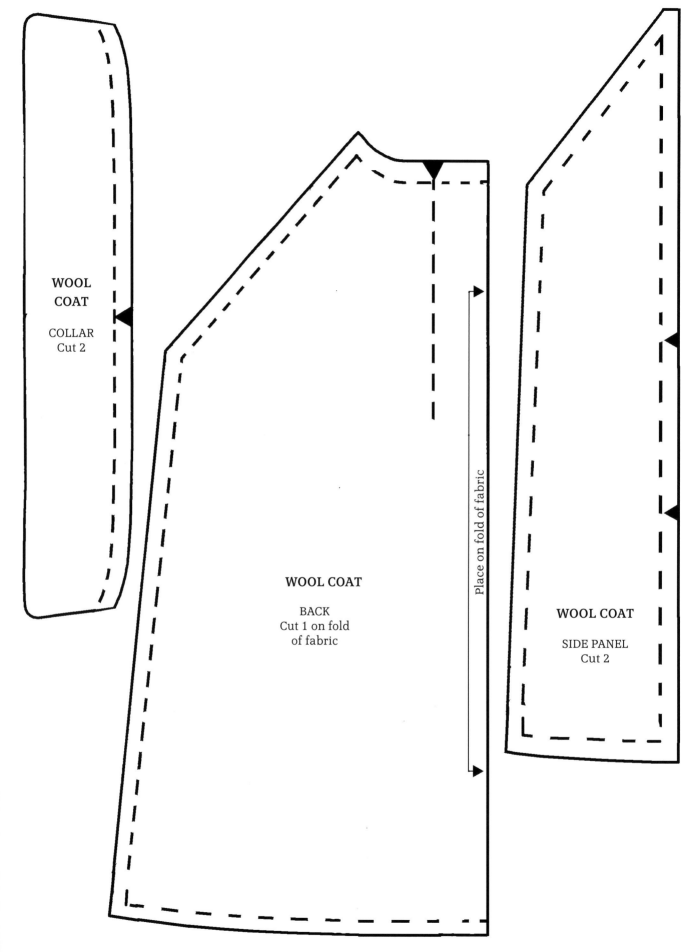

WOOL COAT

COLLAR
Cut 2

WOOL COAT

BACK
Cut 1 on fold
of fabric

Place on fold of fabric

WOOL COAT

SIDE PANEL
Cut 2

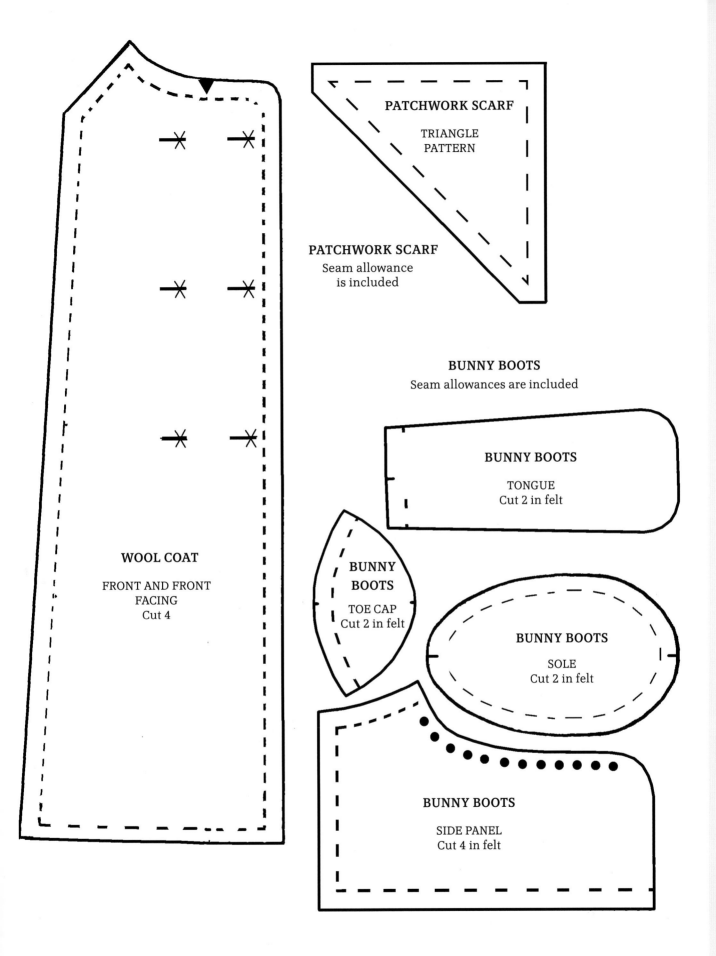

PATCHWORK SCARF

TRIANGLE
PATTERN

PATCHWORK SCARF
Seam allowance
is included

BUNNY BOOTS
Seam allowances are included

BUNNY BOOTS

TONGUE
Cut 2 in felt

**BUNNY
BOOTS**

TOE CAP
Cut 2 in felt

BUNNY BOOTS

SOLE
Cut 2 in felt

WOOL COAT

FRONT AND FRONT
FACING
Cut 4

BUNNY BOOTS

SIDE PANEL
Cut 4 in felt

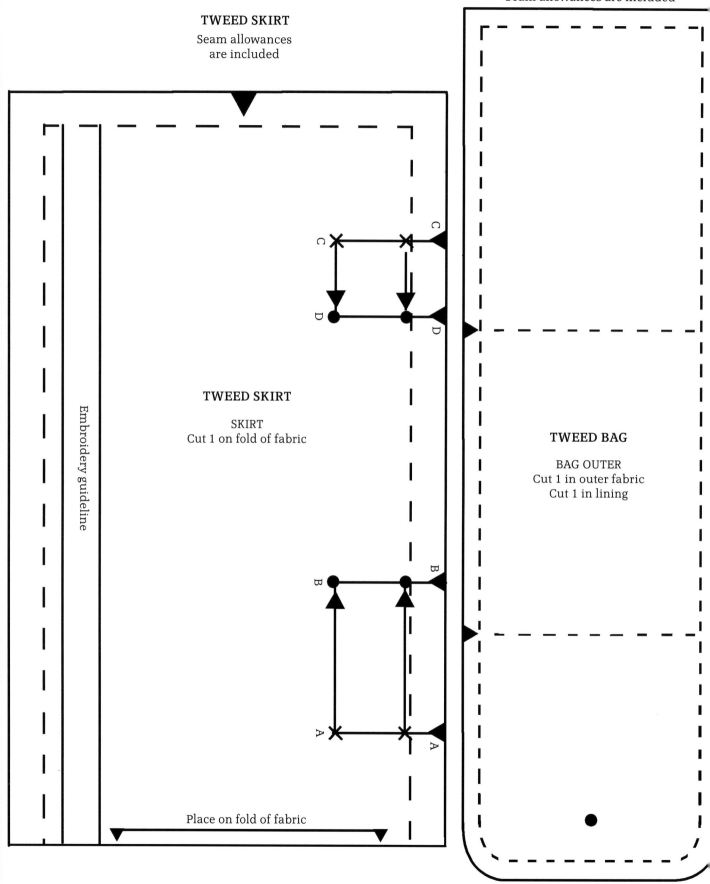

TWEED SKIRT
Seam allowances
are included

TWEED BAG
Seam allowances are included

Embroidery guideline

TWEED SKIRT

SKIRT
Cut 1 on fold of fabric

TWEED BAG

BAG OUTER
Cut 1 in outer fabric
Cut 1 in lining

Place on fold of fabric

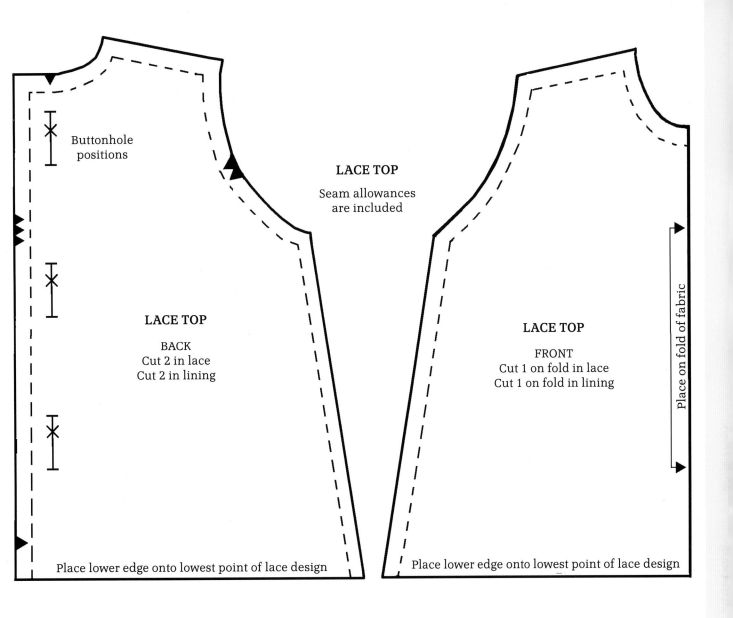

Buttonhole positions

LACE TOP

Seam allowances are included

LACE TOP

BACK
Cut 2 in lace
Cut 2 in lining

LACE TOP

FRONT
Cut 1 on fold in lace
Cut 1 on fold in lining

Place on fold of fabric

Place lower edge onto lowest point of lace design

Place lower edge onto lowest point of lace design

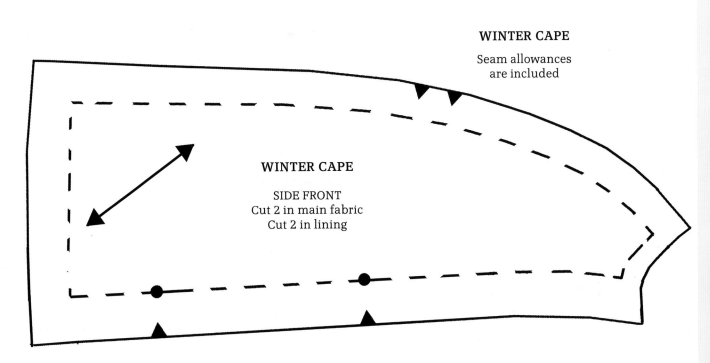

WINTER CAPE

Seam allowances are included

WINTER CAPE

SIDE FRONT
Cut 2 in main fabric
Cut 2 in lining

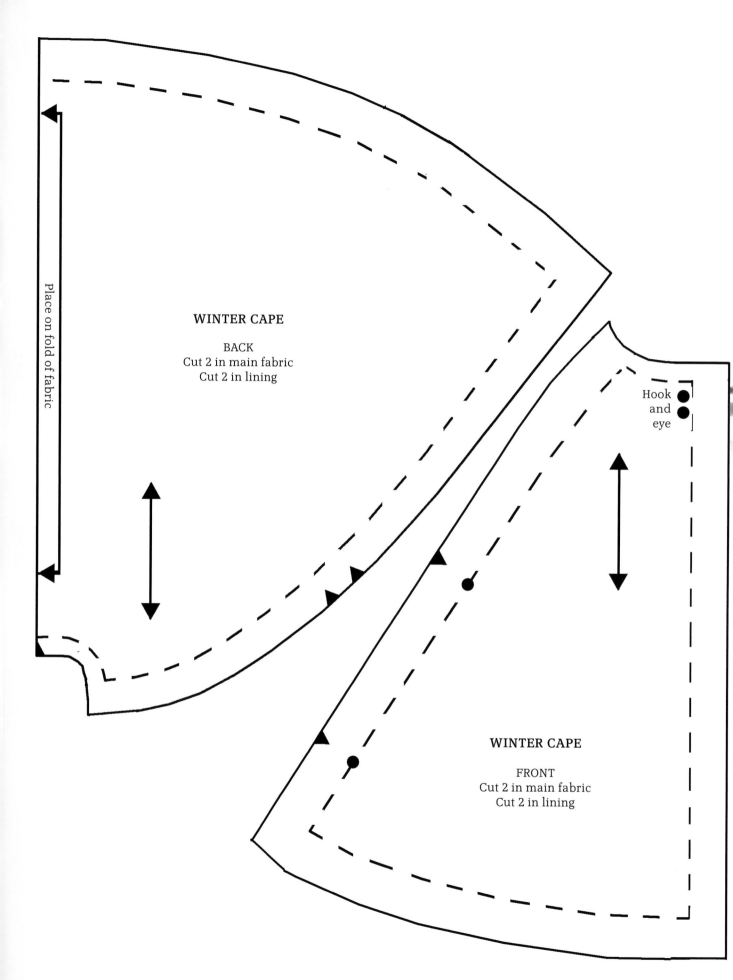

Place on fold of fabric

WINTER CAPE

BACK
Cut 2 in main fabric
Cut 2 in lining

Hook
and
eye

WINTER CAPE

FRONT
Cut 2 in main fabric
Cut 2 in lining

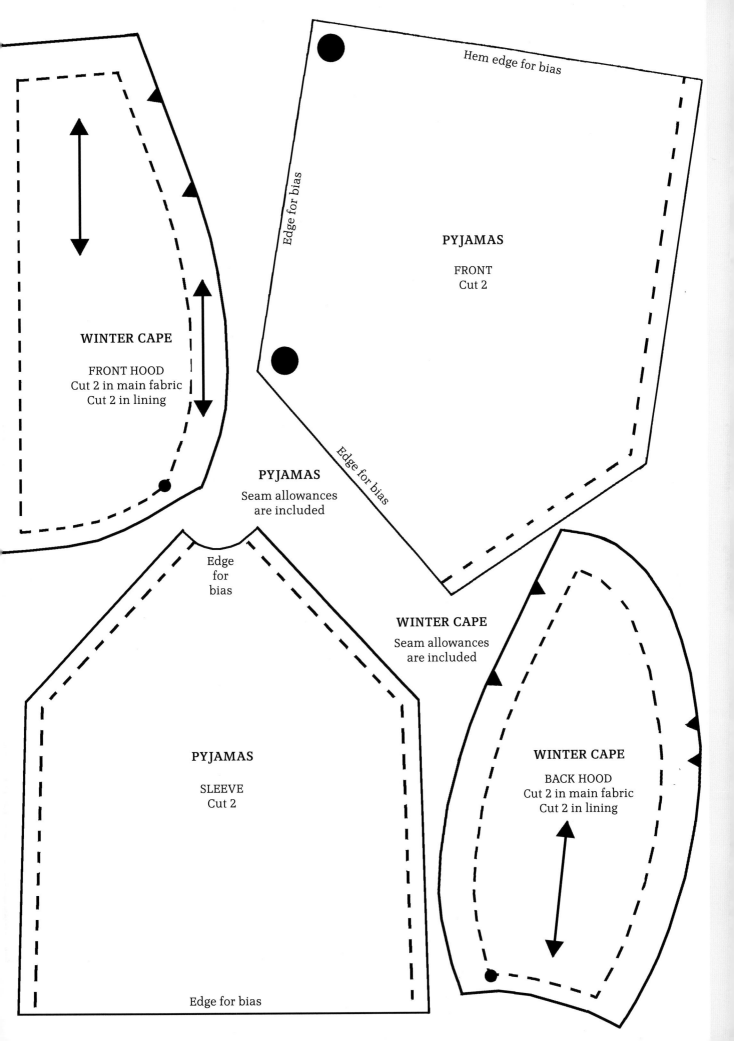

WINTER CAPE

FRONT HOOD
Cut 2 in main fabric
Cut 2 in lining

Hem edge for bias

Edge for bias

PYJAMAS

FRONT
Cut 2

Edge for bias

PYJAMAS

Seam allowances
are included

Edge
for
bias

WINTER CAPE

Seam allowances
are included

PYJAMAS

SLEEVE
Cut 2

WINTER CAPE

BACK HOOD
Cut 2 in main fabric
Cut 2 in lining

Edge for bias

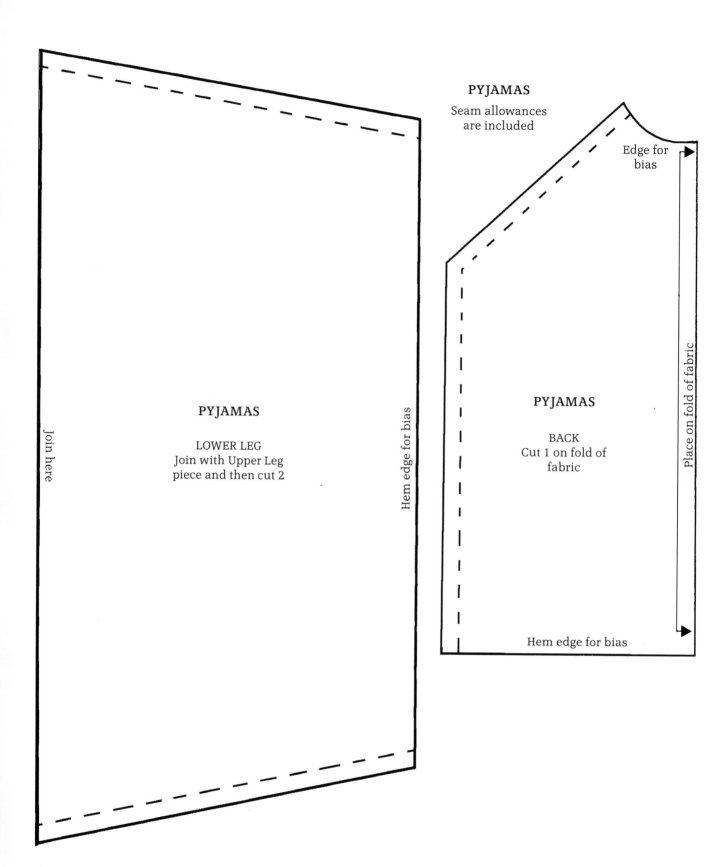

PYJAMAS

LOWER LEG
Join with Upper Leg
piece and then cut 2

Join here

Hem edge for bias

PYJAMAS

Seam allowances
are included

Edge for
bias

PYJAMAS

BACK
Cut 1 on fold of
fabric

Place on fold of fabric

Hem edge for bias

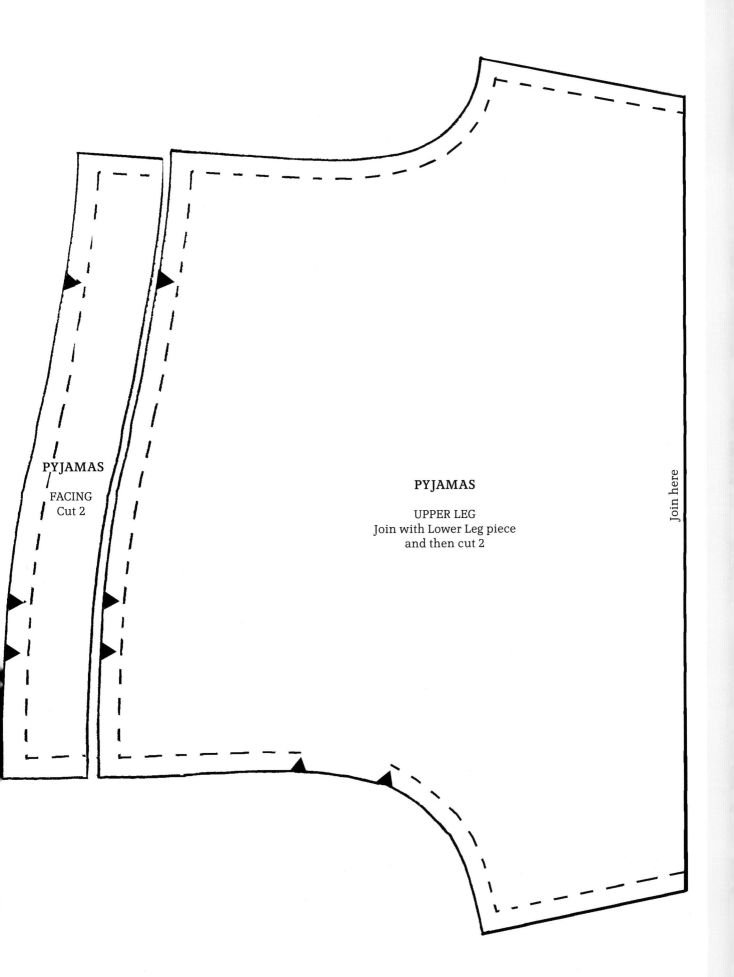

PYJAMAS

FACING
Cut 2

PYJAMAS

UPPER LEG
Join with Lower Leg piece
and then cut 2

Join here

SUPPLIERS

I always like to consider what I have already before I shop, as that way my purchases have more value. So have a look in your stash, consider old clothes that could have a new life, or browse your nearest charity shop. There are a huge amount of suppliers online, and you can also look in your local haberdashery stores for supplies. Most supplies can be bought from coolcrafting.co.uk either individually or as kits for each project.

CoolCrafting
40 Main Street, Kirkby Lonsdale,
Cumbria LA6 2AJ
Tel: 01539 561928
Email: info@coolcrafting.co.uk
www.coolcrafting.co.uk
For a wide range of contemporary craft products, including sewing supplies, print fabrics, wool felt, buttons, ribbons, trims, braids, lace and bias binding (including lace-edged)

There are some supplies that aren't stocked by CoolCrafting but which you may like to consider, as follows.

Tweed
www.fabricaffair.com
For beautiful, washed Irish Donegal tweeds

Liberty Fabrics
www.liberty.co.uk
The home of Tana Lawn prints, which are a perfect scale for Luna's little world

Foam
www.thefoamshop.co.uk
Select your dimensions online for a quote

Toy Stuffing
www.bronteglen.co.uk

ACKNOWLEDGMENTS

Thank you to Joan Peel, my mother – maker of magic – for all those childhood hours in the garden making fairies out of poppy heads with petal dresses.

To Grace Machon, my daughter, for the beautiful stories of Luna, which are interwoven in this book. They are what make the pages talk to me.

To my boys, Nathan and Callum who have learnt to live with a very untidy house and a lack of food in the pantry whilst I have been nurturing the CoolCrafting business.

To my partner, Anthony for doing the driving to shows and workshops across Britain, for singing to me with his beautiful voice and bearing with me through all of this.

To Sheila Mason, world-class stitcher and friend who has made more Lunas and more of her tiny clothes than I dare to think about.

To Lin Clements, project editor of this book, for her diligence and guidance in putting this book together.

ABOUT THE AUTHOR

CoolCrafting founder Sarah Peel has a lifetime of experience within the fashion industry. Sensing a movement back to 'handmade', Sarah set up the business in 2011, providing inspirational workshops, supplies and kits for sewing and crafting. She lives on the edge of the English Lake District in Hincaster, Cumbria with her family, dog and cat. Luna was born on a dark, Christmassy night in 2013 and is now a huge part of the business. As well as selling online, Sarah opened the first CoolCrafting shop in Kirkby Lonsdale, Cumbria in 2015.

www.coolcrafting.co.uk

INDEX

A DAVID & CHARLES BOOK
© F&W Media International, Ltd 2016

David & Charles is an imprint of F&W Media International, Ltd
Pynes Hill Court, Pynes Hill, Exeter, EX2 5AZ, UK

F&W Media International, Ltd is a subsidiary of F+W Media, Inc
10151 Carver Road, Suite #200, Blue Ash, OH 45242, USA

Text and Designs © Sarah Peel 2016
Short Stories © Grace Machon 2016
Layout and Photography © F&W Media International, Ltd 2016

First published in the UK and USA in 2016
Sarah Peel has asserted her right to be identified as author of this work in accordance
with the Copyright, Designs and Patents Act, 1988.

A catalogue record for this book is available from the British Library.

ISBN-13: 978-1-4463-0625-3 paperback
ISBN-10: 1-4463-0625-9 paperback
ISBN-13: 978-1-4463-7418-4 PDF
ISBN-10: 1-4463-7418-1 PDF
ISBN-13: 978-1-4463-7417-7 EPUB
ISBN-10: 1-4463-7417-3 EPUB

Printed in the UK by Latimer Trend for:
F&W Media International, Ltd
Pynes Hill Court, Pynes Hill, Exeter, EX2 5AZ, UK

10 9 8 7

Acquisitions Editor: Sarah Callard
Desk Editor: Michelle Patten
Editorial Assistant: Emma Fletcher
Project Editor: Linda Clements
Art Editor: Anna Wade
Production Manager: Beverley Richardson
Design, Art Direction and Styling: Prudence Rogers
Photography: Jason Jenkins

F+W Media publishes high quality books on a wide range of
subjects. For more great book ideas visit: www.sewandso.co.uk

Layout of the digital edition of this book may vary
depending on reader hardware and display settings.